Number 151
Fall 2016

New Directions ~~for Evaluation~~

Paul R. Brandon
Editor-in-Chief

Evaluating Student Learning in Higher Education: Beyond the Public Rhetoric

William H. Rickards
Monica Stitt-Bergh
Editors

EVALUATING STUDENT LEARNING IN HIGHER EDUCATION: BEYOND THE PUBLIC RHETORIC
William H. Rickards, Monica Stitt-Bergh (eds.)
New Directions for Evaluation, no. 151
Paul R. Brandon, Editor-in-Chief

Microfilm copies of issues and articles are available in 16mm and 35mm, as well as microfiche in 105mm, through University Microfilms Inc., 300 North Zeeb Road, Ann Arbor, MI 48106-1346.

New Directions for Evaluation is indexed in Academic Search Alumni Edition (EBSCO Publishing), Education Research Complete (EBSCO Publishing), Higher Education Abstracts (Claremont Graduate University), SCOPUS (Elsevier), Social Services Abstracts (ProQuest), Sociological Abstracts (ProQuest), Worldwide Political Science Abstracts (ProQuest).

NEW DIRECTIONS FOR EVALUATION (ISSN 1097-6736, electronic ISSN 1534-875X) is part of The Jossey-Bass Education Series and is published quarterly by Wiley Subscription Services, Inc., A Wiley Company, at Jossey-Bass, One Montgomery Street, Suite 1200, San Francisco, CA 94104-4594.

SUBSCRIPTIONS for individuals cost $89 for U.S./Canada/Mexico/international. For institutions, $358 U.S.; $398 Canada/Mexico; $432 international. Electronic only: $89 for individuals all regions; $358 for institutions all regions. Print and electronic: $98 for individuals in the U.S., Canada, and Mexico; $122 for individuals for the rest of the world; $430 for institutions in the U.S.; $470 for institutions in Canada and Mexico; $504 for institutions for the rest of the world.

All issues are proposed by guest editors. For proposal submission guidelines, go to http://www.eval.org/p/cm/ld/fid=48. Editorial correspondence should be addressed to the Editor-in-Chief, Paul R. Brandon, University of Hawai'i at Mānoa, 1776 University Avenue, Castle Memorial Hall Rm 118, Honolulu, HI 96822-2463.

www.josseybass.com

Cover photograph by ©iStock.com/Smithore

Editorial Policy and Procedures

New Directions for Evaluation, a quarterly sourcebook, is an official publication of the American Evaluation Association. The journal publishes works on all aspects of evaluation, with an emphasis on presenting timely and thoughtful reflections on leading-edge issues of evaluation theory, practice, methods, the profession, and the organizational, cultural, and societal context within which evaluation occurs. Each issue of the journal is devoted to a single topic, with contributions solicited, organized, reviewed, and edited by one or more guest editors.

The editor-in-chief is seeking proposals for journal issues from around the globe about topics new to the journal (although topics discussed in the past can be revisited). A diversity of perspectives and creative bridges between evaluation and other disciplines, as well as chapters reporting original empirical research on evaluation, are encouraged. A wide range of topics and substantive domains are appropriate for publication, including evaluative endeavors other than program evaluation; however, the proposed topic must be of interest to a broad evaluation audience.

Journal issues may take any of several forms. Typically they are presented as a series of related chapters, but they might also be presented as a debate; an account, with critique and commentary, of an exemplary evaluation; a feature-length article followed by brief critical commentaries; or perhaps another form proposed by guest editors.

Submitted proposals must follow the format found via the Association's website at http://www.eval.org/Publications/NDE.asp. Proposals are sent to members of the journal's Editorial Advisory Board and to relevant substantive experts for single-blind peer review. The process may result in acceptance, a recommendation to revise and resubmit, or rejection. The journal does not consider or publish unsolicited single manuscripts.

Before submitting proposals, all parties are asked to contact the editor-in-chief, who is committed to working constructively with potential guest editors to help them develop acceptable proposals. For additional information about the journal, see the "Statement of the Editor-in-Chief" in the Spring 2013 issue (No. 137).

Paul R. Brandon, Editor-in-Chief
University of Hawai'i at Mānoa
College of Education
1776 University Avenue
Castle Memorial Hall, Rm. 118
Honolulu, HI 968222463
e-mail: nde@eval.org

CONTENTS

EDITORS' NOTES

Formal evaluation of U.S. colleges and universities only recently has included information on what students learn and how much they know. As the regional and professional accrediting organizations and the U.S. Department of Education have increasingly demanded that institutions provide evidence of student learning, public reports have questioned whether that learning was adequate in articles such as "Your So-Called Education" (Arum & Roksa, 2011b) and "The Fundamental Way that Universities Are an Illusion" (Carey, 2015) and books like *Academically Adrift* (Arum & Roksa, 2011a). Agendas that reflect a testing and accountability viewpoint have been proposed (e.g., U.S. Department of Education, 2006), fueled in part by the cost of a college education and poor completion rates (see the National Center for Education Statistics, 2015, for recent data). These agendas distract from the extensiveness of higher education's use of evaluation practices to improve student learning and educational effectiveness. Evaluators can help educators and policy makers see past the rhetoric and bring more accurate understanding of postsecondary learning through fundamental and emerging practices—particularly the interactions between evaluators and faculty members.

In this issue of *New Directions for Evaluation* (NDE), we focus on U.S. colleges' and universities' practices to evaluate what students know and can do as a result of an academic program—that is, beyond any individual course. In the higher education literature, thought leaders refer to this as *learning outcomes assessment*; in evaluation terminology, it is utilization-focused outcome evaluation with goals that include program/organization improvement and an integration of evaluative thinking in the program and organization. The widespread, mandated learning outcomes assessment at the level of the academic program has resulted in the interaction and further development of methods and processes that involve complex attention to faculty learning.

The contributors to this NDE issue delve into the inner workings of assessment at North American institutions of higher education and reveal new opportunities for evaluators and for the study of evaluation in context. They describe how practices in evaluation (such as capacity building) are being applied at colleges and universities and the challenges that evaluators face in this context. The contributors place importance on the evaluators' capacity to support the deliberative work of faculty, staff, and administrators, a process equally as important as managing the technical aspects of learning outcomes assessment. These chapters offer new perspectives on how to prepare evaluators for assessment in higher education, from improving measurement expertise to communication strategies that support the

NEW DIRECTIONS FOR EVALUATION, no. 151, Fall 2016 © 2016 Wiley Periodicals, Inc., and the American Evaluation Association. Published online in Wiley Online Library (wileyonlinelibrary.com) • DOI: 10.1002/ev.20194 discourse of educators. Assessment in higher education speaks to the evaluation field more generally in terms of those who support evaluation inquiry within other advanced fields of expertise (e.g., legal services, medicine, mental health, and law enforcement).

Brief Overview of the Chapters

The contributors to this NDE issue present nine examinations of evaluation practice that explore different approaches and difficulties using evaluation inquiry to support academic programs. We open with an overview of assessment in higher education, in which we describe the context, impetus, and primary challenges facing evaluators when tackling learning outcomes assessment. In Chapter 2, Beverly Parsons, Chris Lovato, Kylie Hutchinson, and Derek Wilson outline a *community-of-practice* model designed to foster and sustain an evaluative inquiry process and use it as a critical lens in order to provide recommendations for success. This chapter presents a relatively mature version of a collaborative evaluation practice integrated in the educational practices of two institutions. The next four chapters address specific aspects and contexts of evaluation practice in higher education. In Chapter 3, John F. Stevenson, Sandy Jean Hicks, and Anne Hubbard examine the evaluators' roles when assessing a program (general education) that has many stakeholders, competing demands, and changing organizational leadership. In Chapter 4, William Rickards, Jeana Abromeit, Marcia Mentkowski, and Heather Mernitz examine the evaluation of an assessment used midway in an undergraduate program to address the development of quantitative literacy, concentrating on engaging faculty in using evaluation results. In Chapter 5, Monica Stitt-Bergh studies the effect of a multiyear evaluation capacity-building initiative that involves highly skilled experts (faculty) who are generally reluctant to engage in assessment. In Chapter 6, Aaron Tesch highlights the complexities and advantages of outcomes assessment in a pretest/posttest design and the use of results at different levels in the organization.

The next two chapters examine more fundamental concerns in the conduct of higher education evaluations. In Chapter 7, Charles Secolsky, Clare Sng, Ellen Wentland, and Dwight L. Smith III bring to light particular measurement issues that arise in learning outcomes assessment and offer suggestions to facilitate communication between the clients (faculty) and the evaluator. In Chapter 8, David Eubanks and David Gliem apply validity as a framework to address the need for credible and meaningful evidence in learning outcomes assessment and the importance of keeping stakeholders such as employers in mind. In Chapter 9, we, along with Tamara Bertrand Jones, conclude by summarizing the themes, evaluation challenges and responses, and the developing role of evaluators as they serve institutions engaged in studying their own educational practices.

New Directions for Evaluation • DOI: 10.1002/ev

References

Arum, R., & Roksa, J. (2011a). *Academically adrift: Limited learning on college campuses.* Chicago, IL: University of Chicago Press.

Arum, R., & Roksa, J. (2011b, May 14). Your so-called education. *New York Times.* Retrieved from http://www.nytimes.com/2011/05/15/opinion/15arum.html

Carey, K. (2015, July 23). The fundamental way that universities are an illusion. *New York Times.* Retrieved from http://www.nytimes.com/2015/07/24/upshot/the-fundamental-way-that-universities-are-an-illusion.html

National Center for Education Statistics. (2015, May). *Institutional retention and graduation rates for undergraduate students.* Retrieved from https://nces.ed.gov/programs/coe/indicator_cva.asp

U.S. Department of Education. (2006, September). *A test of leadership: Charting the future of U.S. higher education.* Washington, DC: Author.

William H. Rickards
Monica Stitt-Bergh
Editors

WILLIAM H. RICKARDS *is a consultant at Independent Evaluation Inquiry.*

MONICA STITT-BERGH *is an associate specialist of assessment at the University of Hawai'i at Mānoa.*

Rickards, W. H., & Stitt-Bergh, M. (2016). Higher education evaluation, assessment, and faculty engagement In W. H. Rickards & M. Stitt-Bergh (Eds.), *Evaluating student learning in higher education: Beyond the public rhetoric. New Directions for Evaluation, 151,* 11–20.

1

Higher Education Evaluation, Assessment, and Faculty Engagement

William H. Rickards, Monica Stitt-Bergh

Abstract

Evaluative practice has a long and deep history in higher education. It has been a persistent part of instructional practice and curriculum, intricately entwined with scholarly efforts to address teaching and learning. From public policy and oversight perspectives, the questions of value and worth have often focused on inputs—faculty credentials, facilities, etc.—as well as fiscal responsibility. But in the last 30 years, attention has turned to student learning as a critical outcome and the assessment of learning as a principal endeavor. The developments in higher education assessment have involved increasingly sophisticated psychometric approaches to measurement as well as more teacherly orientations to the implementation of educational assessments within the individual contexts— and intentions—of colleges and universities. In this chapter, we introduce some of the issues in the field and argue that evaluation has a unique history that is committed to systematically bringing evidence of program outcomes and processes into the discourse of educators—administrators, faculty, and staff—as they examine and build on their own operations. We briefly review the current context and challenges and support increased evaluator–faculty collaboration. We make a case for how the analysis of evaluation practices in higher education is both a means to increasing expertise in those applications and to thinking about evaluation practices across developing and complex institutions. © 2016 Wiley Periodicals, Inc., and the American Evaluation Association.

D uring the last 30 years in the United States, attention to accountability has led to widespread assessment of learning at the program and degree level, which is a new direction for faculty and administrators in higher education. The questions of what learning is expected, what instruments should be used to measure learning, and what evaluation practices drive changes and improvement are up for debate. Some of the public rhetoric presents an argument that academic programs are not adequately attending to student learning and that increased attention to testing would provide evidence that would result in educational transformation (Zemsky, 2007; see also Chambliss, 2007, and Secretary of Education's Commission on the Future of Higher Education, 2006). Other narratives based on extensive research locate the advance of student learning in the context of curriculum and the operation of academic units. These express equal concern about learning but emphasize the interaction of instruction, curriculum, and organizational process:

- Documentation of effective educational practice (Kuh, Kinzie, Schuh, Whitt, & Associates, 2005; Project DEEP, n.d.)
- Kezar's (2014) research on how colleges change, the role of leadership, and organizational processes
- Critical faculty engagement (Banta & Pike, 2012b)
- Use of student learning evidence to improve higher education (Kuh et al., 2015)

It can be useful to understand the interaction of three different perspectives in higher education discourse: (a) broad public concerns that are played out in national funding and policy decisions; (b) policies and practices at the institutional level (and with campus systems such as resources for evaluation and assessment staff that make complicated assessments feasible); and (c) educator perspectives that provide the context in which faculty and departments examine teaching and learning to make meaning out of available data on outcomes. It is in this context of multiple, sometimes competing, perspectives, and narratives on student learning that we describe learning outcomes assessment and the role of evaluation and evaluators.

Furthermore, in implementation, educators are regularly involved in a three-way dynamic that complicates evaluation and operation: data on student learning seldom have meaning in themselves; in the absence of interpretation and meaning making, data collection can be a distracting and expensive activity. Utilization requires a robust, cyclical relationship between *data* (student performance and educational outcomes) and the *meaning-making* activities in which faculty examine their practice and student outcomes, evaluate their principles and practices, make program decisions, and engage in *praxis* (the conduct of services in the educational contexts). Within this constellation of *data, meaning-making* and *praxis*, the roles of the

Figure 1.1. Conceptualizing Evaluation and Utilization in a Community of Educators

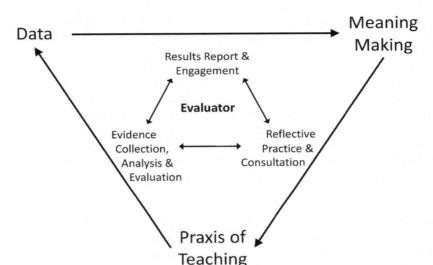

evaluator fundamentally involve a collaborating narrative, explicating the relationships and the processes (e.g., how data are reported and used by faculty to confirm and challenge principles and practices). In particular, this emphasizes the importance of the critical perspective of faculty and their role in meaning making, rather than presuming that data or outcomes have an automatic impact on practice (Figure 1.1). Although these dynamics—*policy, institutional applications, educator concerns,* and *data, meaning making, praxis*—are drafted here in higher education terms, they are frequently at the heart of evaluative reasoning more generally (cf., evaluation-specific logic, Davidson, 2014). Thus, these dynamics become unifying and interpretive considerations in the sections to follow.

Assessment in Higher Education

In the higher education literature, thought leaders use the term *assessment* (not *evaluation*) to describe the "systematic collection, review, and use of information about educational programs undertaken for the purpose of improving student learning and development" (Palomba & Banta, 1999, p. 4). The emphasis is on the program, which sets it apart from other common forms of educational evaluation such as grading individual students. Furthermore, accrediting organizations require that colleges and universities evaluate actual student performances or products (e.g., written papers, examinations, and oral presentations), and they state that survey instruments that gather student perceptions and self-reports are helpful but insufficient evidence of learning. Although advocates argue that faculty and campuses

NEW DIRECTIONS FOR EVALUATION • DOI: 10.1002/ev

should conduct assessment because it is beneficial, the reality is they often conduct and report on assessment because they must do so.

Regional and professional accrediting agencies require that faculty are involved in regular interpretive activities in which data on student learning are used in curriculum review and program decision making. All but one regional accreditor explicitly states that faculty be involved in the assessment processes (Provezis, 2010). This orientation eventually brings the evaluative analysis into the basic faculty planning processes regardless of faculty readiness or level of engagement and raises questions about how assessment and reporting might be used to advance intradepartmental discourse. In response, colleges and universities have increased the resources devoted to improving teaching and learning through assessment activities. Most research universities that took part in the Association of American Universities (2013) survey reported having a newly created office or a newly assigned person specifically responsible for student learning assessment compared to 5 years ago. Across the United States, evaluators have new opportunities in offices of evaluation, assessment, and educational effectiveness. Institutions have changed criteria for program review and new program proposals. They are spending funds on cloud-based assessment management software (e.g., Academic Effect, LiveText, Taskstream, and Tk20) and externally developed tests to meet accreditation requirements (e.g., ACT's Collegiate Assessment of Academic Proficiency, the Council for Aid to Education's Collegiate Learning Assessment, and Educational Testing Service's HEIghten Outcomes Assessment Suite). Philanthropic funding is now available to support organizations such as the National Institute for Learning Outcomes Assessment and initiatives such as the Multi-state Collaborative to Advance Learning Outcomes Assessment and the Valid Assessment of Learning in Undergraduate Education. Assessment leaders, educators, and accreditors have been writing books, organizing conferences and conference tracks/interest groups, and facilitating assessment academies. The growth in the last 30 years has been tremendous and provides evaluators with more employment options and more venues in which to study evaluation in context.

The history of the higher education "assessment movement" has been written about extensively, and we refer interested readers to texts such as *Learner-Centered Assessment on College Campuses* (Huba & Freed, 2000) and *Student Outcomes Assessment: A Historical Review and Guide to Program Development* (Sims, 1992), as well as Ewell (2002, 2008) and Wright (2002). From this history, we highlight the tension between assessment for accountability (external use of findings) and assessment for improving learning (internal use). The former is rooted in using standardized measurements to judge and compare colleges and universities. It promotes reductive accountability models that contribute to simplistic judgments and comparisons across institutions with radically different student populations and missions. (The latter comes from educational reform advocates seeking a shift in focus from what professors teach to what students learn (e.g., Barr & Tagg, 1995; Huba & Freed, 2000; Study Group on the Conditions of Excellence in American Higher Education, 1984). It is formative and relies on internal reporting that presumes that faculty will use indicators of student learning to examine teaching and program concerns. A small number of colleges have a model in which assessment is regarded as a critical element in learning—that is, in performance, the learner makes a critical transfer to different situations that both consolidates and demonstrates the learning (cf., Abate, Stamatakis, & Haggett, 2003; Alverno College Faculty, 1994; Seaba, 2010).

These approaches have different implications for assessment and evaluators' practices. Assessment for accountability—a compliance-based model—locates the evaluation work outside of departmental discourse and inquiry. Evaluators use technologies that have been historically anchored in test and measurement traditions that can relatively quickly address concerns for substantial data and cross-institution comparisons. These tests, created by an external entity, are far from professors and classrooms, and they are fraught with issues related to validity, student motivation, and professor willingness to use findings in curricular decision making. Thus, the evaluators find themselves increasingly concerned with how judgments on student learning become part of the institutional and educational discourse on teaching and learning.

Evaluators who privilege assessment for improvement turn to a practice that integrates traditional measurement-oriented approaches with more participatory, deliberative, and developmental orientations to meet the needs of multiple stakeholders and satisfy both external accountability and internal improvement goals. Frequently cited examples in this area include the use of comprehensive exams or projects completed at program's end as performances that can be subject to an integrated analysis to examine overall program effectiveness, as well as specific elements (Segers, Dochy, & Cascallar, 2003). There are also examples of more structured action research projects focusing on a program's students for assessment and evaluation purposes. By sampling case studies of individual students or selecting specific assessments for departmental review, faculty can synthesize data in ways that serve a whole department in a critical analysis of program performance (Lava, Lehman, & Traugh, 2005). Campuses and evaluators may also use constructivist/mixed method approaches that combine performance assessment, available records, and qualitative approaches in order to address the realistic and complex needs of educators and academic units. Multiple measures along with tracking learning over time are two recommended practices in educational evaluation systems (American Evaluation Association, 2006).

Evaluation models that emphasize stakeholder perspectives and invest in structures of judgment that explicate indicators of value and worth can foster structures of meaning making that are essential to the interpretation of evidence and true accountability. It is a development-based approach that involves dynamic and collaborative approaches in which evaluators and educators cooperate to carry out evaluation inquiry to move educational practices forward.

Evaluation models hold promise for assessment in higher education. Interestingly, the assessment literature and the evaluation literature have not intersected and would benefit from closer connections. For example, assessment experts do not often reference utilization-focused evaluation, evaluation capacity building, or theory of change and they do not acknowledge common tools such as the logic model. Evaluators and the field have much to offer higher education.

Challenges

Many challenges in evaluation cut across sectors: negative reactions, lack of leadership support, confusion about roles and purpose, inadequate resources, too much data to manage, confusion over how to analyze and use information, findings not used, etc. These challenges exist in higher education too, but we concentrate on several particular to education.

First, the issue of ethical treatment of college students is frequently raised. The U.S. federal regulations (Protection of Human Subjects policy and the Family Educational Rights and Privacy Act) are not barriers to assessment projects that involve standard education practice and use of results for internal improvement. However, individual faculty and departments may perceive them as obstacles. Their questions about ethical treatment and the protection of student information can derail a well-designed plan because of decreased participation, loss of trust between those with the student work and those collecting it, and because an insistence on anonymity hinders use of results (confidentiality is advised). Review by an institutional review board (IRB) and student informed consent are not required. Learning outcomes assessment does not meet a key criterion that triggers IRB review: assessment is not research "designed to develop or contribute to generalizable knowledge" (Protection of Human Subjects, 1991, section 46.102(d)). Informed consent is also not a requirement and the Family Educational Rights and Privacy Act (1974) allows transfer of student information between parties with legitimate interests. Because the concern for students is justified, colleges and universities need to engage in regular methods to protect student privacy and inform students of how the institution will use their work and data.

A second challenge is negative reaction by some faculty. The professors (i.e., program staff) in academic programs have publicly put forth more negative press than staff in any other sector in which program evaluation is common. Their message is clear from their article titles, for example, "The Great Assessment Diversion" (Kelly-Woessner, 2011) and "Outcomes Assessment: No Gain, All Pain" (Fryshman, 2007). Professors point to a lack of proof that assessment activities lead to improvement as seen in Gilbert's 2015 piece, "Does Assessment Make Colleges Better? Who Knows?" and to concerns related to validity and reliability such as Hales's 2013 article, "Who's Assessing the Assessors' Assessors?" The external mandate for assessment is one impetus for these negative articles; Powell (2011) sums up much of the critics' positions:

> Outcomes assessment is an odd business. It is not to the credit of higher education that we have tolerated this external assault on our work. Its origins are suspect, its justifications abjure the science we would ordinarily require, it demands enormous efforts for very little payoff, it renounces wisdom, it requires yielding to misunderstandings, and it displaces and distracts us from more urgent tasks, like the teaching and learning it would allegedly help. (p. 21)

Vocal groups of professors have not embraced the assessment movement and some are in positions of power that stall and derail even the most optimistic advocate or well-intentioned evaluator. The negative reaction leads to a lack of engagement and reluctance to use findings, which runs counter to an assessment for improvement model that relies on collaborative participation in evaluative practice. Evaluators contemplating a move into learning outcomes assessment need to be prepared for typical evaluation challenges and also for the sometimes blatant criticism of assessment, the reluctance to engage, and the other demands on faculty time as a result of decreases in education funding.

Third, the nature of the college context presents challenges to inquiry. Most student evaluation processes in college courses are developed by professors for specific course purposes. For program- and institutional-level assessment, data from course evaluations can be aggregated and used to address broader questions of student learning—termed in the assessment literature "embedded assessment"—and this can add to the complexity of analyses. Student achievement, can be reevaluated after a change in practice (e.g., a new course, innovative technologies) to increase outcome achievement, but it will often involve between-group designs complicated by other variables (e.g., student demographics, course taking patterns, and sample size). As in other educational settings and types of educational evaluation, randomized control trials are extremely challenging, if not impossible, to implement.

Learning From and Through Evaluation Practice in Higher Education

The results of assessment efforts have shown familiar characteristics in the developing professional practice of evaluation. Continued debates about what constitutes value and merit and evidence have often been contentious (cf., Davidson, 2010). And the question of appropriate use of learning outcome assessment results becomes particularly significant in higher education (Banta & Pike, 2012a, 2012b). Indeed, just as in K–12 education, higher education faculty can have difficulties with conversations about data in the context of their own curriculum practices.

In the midst of current educational changes and evolving priorities, evaluators are finding ways to support public conversations about the worth and outcomes of higher education while contributing to the substantive educational concerns regarding learning, curriculum, and faculty expertise. This creates multiple tensions on the evaluators' work to provide dashboard indicators and maintain the expert meaning making of faculty who are guiding the coursework and curriculum. This means that evaluators need to understand and appreciate the discourse of those who use evaluative data—in this case, faculty—and work side by side to create trustworthy and meaningful assessments that enhance the educational program. Evaluators seek to anticipate how evaluation's multiple roles are having emerging impact in continuing development in pedagogy, curriculum, and equity and enrollment. To do so, they pay attention to the relationships developing between themselves and faculty and administrators and framing evaluation studies in existing, ongoing work of educational practice. In this regard, they are often challenged by situations where initiative and leadership seem critical to keeping the evaluation discussions evolving, even when these have been less recognized as part of evaluation practice. Because of this, higher education has been a context in which evaluation has made unique contributions and from which evaluation practices can be enhanced through continued development.

For example, this challenges a conceptualization of evaluation in which a singular study provides the fuel for data-driven decision making. Evaluation is an integrative activity in which value, merit, and evidence are used in complex and developmental activities to validate and inform, to think through and rethink our shared endeavors. In these activities, faculty, staff, and administrators become coinvestigators. Although evaluators may be charged with particular parts of study design, data collection, analysis, and certain levels of interpretation, it is the faculty who interpret outcomes into implementation. A sample of recent evaluation studies in higher education gives some insight into what higher education asks of evaluators and, in this regard, offers some insight to contexts in which evaluators work collaboratively with faculty and program staff to interpret program performance and to support ongoing development.

In conclusion, various forms of evaluation have long existed in higher education, but renewed attention to accountability has focused the spotlight on what students know and can do upon graduation (as well as on cost, access, and graduation rates, which are related to learning and teaching). Individual course grades, final grade point averages, and surveys of students' perceptions are now inadequate. Although new evaluation positions have been created and faculty access to evaluation expertise has increased,

NEW DIRECTIONS FOR EVALUATION • DOI: 10.1002/ev

pressure to conduct assessment often leadsfaculty to go it on their own as "accidental evaluators." Thus, evaluators and participatory and collaborative evaluation approaches can help colleges and universities conduct better outcomes assessment. Subsequent research on evaluation in the higher education context can inform the field of evaluation, particularly other sectors with highly skilled professionals can benefit from studies of evaluators working with faculty experts who live in disciplinary subcultures.

References

Abate, M. A., Stamatakis, M. K., & Haggett, R. R. (2003). Excellence in curriculum development and assessment. *American Journal of Pharmaceutical Education.* 67(3), 1–22.

Alverno College Faculty. (1994). *Student assessment-as-learning at Alverno College* (3rd ed.). Milwaukee, WI: Alverno College.

American Evaluation Association. (2006, November 1). *Public statement: Educational accountability*. Retrieved from http://www.eval.org/p/cm/ld/fid=94

Association of American Universities. (2013). *Top research universities expanding efforts to assess, improve undergraduate student learning*. Washington DC: Author, Retrieved from http://www.aau.edu/WorkArea/DownloadAsset.aspx?id=14849

Banta, T. W., & Pike, G. R. (2012a). Making the case against—one more time. In R. Benjamin (Ed.), *The seven red herrings about standardized assessment in higher education* (NILOA Occasional Paper No. 15, pp. 24–30). Urbana, IL: University of Illinois and Indiana University, National Institute for Learning Outcomes Assessment.

Banta, T. W., & Pike, G. R. (2012b). The bottom line: Will faculty USE assessment findings? In C. Secolsky & D. B. Dennison (Eds.), *Handbook on measurement, assessment, and evaluation in higher education* (pp. 47–56). New York, NY: Routledge.

Barr, R., & Tagg, J. (1995). From teaching to learning—A new paradigm for undergraduate education. *Change: The Magazine of Higher Learning.* 27(6), 13–25.

Chambliss, D. F. (2007, April 5). The flawed metaphor of the Spellings summit. *Inside Higher Education*. Retrieved from https://www.insidehighered.com/views/2007/04/05/chambliss

Davidson, J. (2010, December 9). Pushing sand uphill with a pointy stick? "No value-free" in higher ed evaluation [Web log post]. Retrieved from http://genuineevaluation.com/pushing-sand-uphill-with-a-pointy-stick-no-value-free-in-higher-ed-evaluation/

Davidson, J. (2014). *Evaluative Reasoning, Methodological Briefs: Impact Evaluation 4*. Florence: UNICEF.

Ewell, P. T. (2002). An emerging scholarship: A brief history of assessment. In T. W. Banta & Associates (Eds.), *Building a scholarship of assessment* (pp. 3–25). San Francisco, CA: Jossey-Bass.

Ewell, P. T. (2008). Assessment and accountability in America today: Background and context. In V. M. H. Borden & G. R. Pike (Eds.), *New Directions for Institutional Research: No. S1. Assessing and accounting for student learning: Beyond the Spellings Commission* (pp. 7–18). San Francisco, CA: Jossey-Bass

Family Educational Rights and Privacy Act of 1974, 20 C.F.R. §1232g et seq.

Fryshman, B. (2007, November 13). Outcomes assessment: No gain, all pain. *Inside Higher Education*. Retrieved from https://www.insidehighered.com/views/2007/11/13/fryshman

Gilbert, E. (2015, August 15). Does assessment make colleges better? Who knows? *Chronicle of Higher Education*. Retrieved from http://chronicle.com/article/Does-Assessment-Make-Colleges/232371/

Hales, S. (2013, March 11). Who's assessing the assessors' assessors? *Chronicle of Higher Education*. Retrieved from http://chronicle.com/article/Whos-Assessing-the-Assessors/137829/

Huba, M. E., & Freed, J. E. (2000). *Learner-centered assessment on college campuses: Shifting the focus from teaching to learning*. Needham Heights, MA: Allyn & Bacon.

Kelly-Woessner, A. (2011, February 13). The great assessment diversion. *Chronicle of Higher Education*. Retrieved from http://chronicle.com/article/The-Great-Assessment-Diversion/126347/

Kezar, A. (2014). *How colleges change: Understanding, leading, and enacting change*. New York, NY: Routledge.

Kuh, G. D., Ikenberry, S. O., Jankowski, N. A., Cain, T. R., Ewell, P. T., Hutchings, P., & Kinzie, J. (2015). *Using evidence of student learning to improve higher education*. San Francisco: Wiley & Sons.

Kuh, G. D., Kinzie, J., Schuh, J. H., & Whitt, E. J., & Associates. (2005). *Student success in college: Creating conditions that matter*. Washington DC: American Association for Higher Education.

Lava, V., Lehman, L, & Traugh, C. (2005). Re-imagining one urban teacher education program: Transformation through inquiry, difference and field experience. In P. M. Jenlink & K. E. Jenlink (Eds.), *Portraits of teacher preparation: Learning to teach in a changing America* (pp. 73–94). Lanham, MD: Rowman & Littlefield Education.

Palomba, C. A., & Banta, T. W. (1999). *Assessment essentials*. San Francisco, CA: Jossey-Bass.

Powell, J. W. (2011). Outcomes assessment: Conceptual and other problems. *AAUP Journal of Academic Freedom*. 2(2), 1–25.

Project DEEP: Documenting effective educational practice. (n.d.). Retrieved from http://nsse.indiana.edu/html/projectDEEP.cfm

Protection of Human Subjects. (1991). 45 C.F.R. §46 et seq.

Provezis, S. (2010). *Regional accreditation and student learning outcomes: Mapping the territory*. Champaign, IL: National Institute for Learning Outcomes Assessment.

Seaba, H. H. (2010). Assessment in the College of Pharmacy. Retrieved from http://pharmacy.uiowa.edu/files/pharmacy.uiowa.edu/files/wysiwyg_uploads/assessment_in_the_college_of_pharmacy_1999-2010.pdf

Secretary of Education's Commission on the Future of Higher Education. (2006). *A test of leadership: Charting the future of U.S. higher education*. Washington, DC: U.S. Department of Education.

Segers, M., Dochy, F., & Cascallar, E. (2003). *Optimising new modes of assessment: In search of qualities and standards*. Dordrecht, The Netherlands: Kluwer Academic.

Sims, S. J. (1992). *Student outcomes assessment: A historical review and guide to program development*. New York, NY: Greenwood Press,

Study Group on the Conditions of Excellence in American Higher Education. (1984). *Involvement in learning: Realizing the potential of American higher education*. Washington, DC: U.S. Department of Education, National Institute of Education. Retrieved from http://files.eric.ed.gov/fulltext/ED246833.pdf

Wright, B. D. (2002). Accreditation and the scholarship of assessment. In *Building a scholarship of assessment* (pp. 240–258). San Francisco, CA: Jossey-Bass.

Zemsky, R. (2007). The rise and fall of the Spellings Commission. *Chronicle of Higher Education*. 53(21), B6.

WILLIAM H. RICKARDS *is a consultant at Independent Evaluation Inquiry.*

MONICA STITT-BERGH *is an associate specialist of assessment at the University of Hawai'i at Mānoa.*

NEW DIRECTIONS FOR EVALUATION • DOI: 10.1002/ev

Parsons, B. L., Lovato, C. Y., Hutchinson, K., & Wilson, D. (2016). Building evaluation capacity through CLIPs: Communities of learning, inquiry, and practice. In W. H. Rickards & M. Stitt-Bergh (Eds.), *Evaluating student learning in higher education: Beyond the public rhetoric. New Directions for Evaluation, 151*, 21–36.

2

Building Evaluation Capacity Through CLIPs: Communities of Learning, Inquiry, and Practice

Beverly L. Parsons, Chris Y. Lovato, Kylie Hutchinson, Derek Wilson

Abstract

This chapter focuses on a model for building evaluation capacity. The approach embeds evaluative thinking and practice into the work of higher education leaders, faculty, and staff who need evidence to guide their planning and decision making. Communities of Learning, Inquiry, and Practice (CLIPs) are a type of community of practice; they are informal, dynamic groups of faculty and staff who inquire and learn together about their professional practice and operate within a support structure specifically designed to fit the higher education context. This chapter describes two institutions in which the CLIPs model was implemented—a community college in the United States and a medical school in Canada. Based on the results from these case examples, seven guiding principles are proposed for implementing successful CLIPs. This model is adaptable to organizations beyond higher education. © 2016 Wiley Periodicals, Inc., and the American Evaluation Association.

The Communities of Learning, Inquiry, and Practice (CLIPs) model was developed within the higher education context under funding from the National Science Foundation (NSF)[1] to support faculty and

[1] The CLIP model development was funded under an NSF grant (# 0335581) to InSites.

staff as they renew their educational practices in times of organizational change. The approach is designed to foster evaluative inquiry and organizational learning by empowering professionals to gather, analyze, and make meaning from data about questions of importance to them. The process is designed to help professionals become comfortable using evaluation to improve practice by building relationships among participants and connecting their work to the bigger purpose and goals of their organization. It embeds evaluative thinking into the practice of the participating professionals, closely links evaluation and practice, is designed to be economically sound, and encourages sustainability of the evaluation capacity-building process.

The CLIPs model was introduced to many community colleges through Achieving the Dream, a national reform network of colleges, state leaders, educators, and others who share the goal of helping community college students succeed (www.achievingthedream.org). Based on our experiences in settings inside and outside of higher education, we believe this capacity-building model can also be adapted for use in nonprofit organizations, government, and private businesses.

In this chapter, we describe variations of the CLIPs model implemented in two postsecondary institutions, one in Canada and the other in the United States. They are two quite different educational settings (a community college and a medical school) and demonstrate, in two different ways, how both internal and external evaluators were involved in guiding the process. Seven guiding principles are suggested and discussed for those who seek to apply the model in their own setting.

Basic CLIP Model

CLIPs are a type of community of practice (Wenger, McDermott, & Snyder, 2002; Wenger & Snyder, 2000). Communities of practice are groups formed to accomplish a purpose valued by all participants. They are driven by a personal desire and professional need to share problems, experiences, insights, tools, and practice. CLIPs are informal, dynamic groups of professionals who learn together about their professional practice and operate within a supportive structure. They are also designed to engage staff, enhance organizational capacity, and focus on learning transfer (Preskill, 2014). The model uses a systems approach by encouraging self-organizing groups in a direction that is consistent with the direction of the organization. At the same time, it facilitates CLIPs participants in identifying questions that are not only relevant to their own work but ones that those leading the organization may not have considered. See Parsons (2009) for more detail about the CLIPs design and link to systems thinking based on the development of the process at Bakersfield College in California.

NEW DIRECTIONS FOR EVALUATION • DOI: 10.1002/ev

Table 2.1. CLIPs Resource Modules*

Module	Description
1. What Are CLIPs	What CLIPs are, how they operate, and the benefits they offer
2. Eight Guiding Principles for CLIPs	Guiding principles for CLIPs groups
3. Designing the CLIP Inquiry	How to determine the purpose of the inquiry, position it among other inquiries and activities, identify the main questions to be addressed, develop a plan to collect information, analyze data, and report data
4. Gather Data for the CLIP Inquiry	How to plan the sources and methods of collecting the data for the inquiry
5. Making Meaning and Shaping Practice	Making meaning from data through analysis and interpretation and sharing results to shape practice
6. Being a CLIP Facilitator	How to fulfill the roles and responsibilities of a CLIPs group facilitator
7. Being a CLIP Guide	How to fulfill the roles and responsibilities of a CLIPs guide

*All modules are available at http://www.insites.org

CLIPs gather and analyze data about a question of importance to them. Participants from multiple groups engage in their own evaluative inquiry process using three basic steps: (a) design the inquiry, (b) collect data, and (c) make meaning and shape practice.

Typically, each CLIP consists of three to seven people who chose a shared inquiry question and project. One of the group members serves as the CLIP facilitator. An overall CLIP guide who has strong evaluation and facilitation expertise supports the work of multiple CLIPs, builds strategic linkages among the groups, and connects the whole process appropriately to the institution's other processes and initiatives. The small groups support, and are supported by, the broader institutional goals.

The basic design has three major components: (a) the work of individual CLIPs, (b) multi-CLIP interactions, and (c) a supporting infrastructure within the organization. The latter two components are especially important in the sustainability of the process in the organization. Table 2.1 summarizes an eight-module participant guide that provides information on the principles, processes, and structure for a CLIPs initiative. The modules developed at Bakersfield College are online and can be downloaded at ⟨http://www.insites.org/⟩. Organizations are encouraged to modify the structures and processes to make them appropriate for their setting.

In the examples presented here, the CLIPs process was specifically designed to fit a postsecondary education context. In the remainder of this chapter, we focus on describing the CLIPs application in Bakersfield College and the University of British Columbia (UBC).

New Directions for Evaluation • DOI: 10.1002/ev

Settings for Two Postsecondary CLIPs Applications

The individual site contexts are important to understanding CLIPs operations.

Bakersfield College. Bakersfield College served as the site for the original CLIPs research and development. It was funded in 2004 through a grant from the NSF to a nonprofit research and evaluation firm that designed and tested the CLIPs approach. Bakersfield College, a 2-year public community college[2] in California's southern San Joaquin Valley, is a federally designated Hispanic-Serving Institution with over 35% Hispanic student enrollment. It is in one of the most economically distressed areas of the state. Bakersfield College is the oldest continually operating community college in the United States. It has about 16,000 students and about 500 contract and adjunct faculty. About half are full-time contract faculty and about half are adjunct faculty. The faculty is unionized and a tenure system exists. The college faces problems of low student retention and persistence, low transfer rates, and low degree completion rates.

Bakersfield College underwent an accreditation review in spring 2005 based on new accreditation standards requiring an outcomes-based approach to instructional programs. The shift toward outcomes was occurring at a time of major budget cuts that were severely limiting faculty development opportunities. In an informal survey, approximately 65% of Bakersfield College's faculty indicated they needed and would participate in instructional training. (An overreliance on lecture methods was a major problem.) Faculty and administrators were already "in motion" toward a redesign of their work and were eager for the external support that the CLIPs process provided for faculty to learn together about ways to improve instruction.

A total of 80 people participated as CLIPs members at Bakersfield College during the study period from 2004–2008. The CLIPs groups conducted 24 studies over 4 years. CLIPs addressed topics such as peer study groups, the success of students who had been in developmental education courses in subsequent courses, and how best to support adjunct faculty. All groups finished their projects and submitted a final product.

The college has an office of institutional research but not an evaluation unit. It has an institutional effectiveness committee and an assessment committee, each composed of about a dozen faculty and administrators (mostly faculty). The CLIPs process provided a structure for enhancing evaluation capacity. The college continued CLIPs for several years after the NSF funding but severe budget cuts results in its eventual elimination.

---

[2] In the United States, community colleges are primarily 2-year public institutions providing higher education courses that can be transferred to 4-year colleges and universities to complete a bachelor's degree. They also offer technical training and grant certificates, diplomas, and associate's degrees. Other countries do not necessarily use the term "community college" for such institutions.

NEW DIRECTIONS FOR EVALUATION • DOI: 10.1002/ev

The CLIPs development process was accompanied by a formative evaluation conducted by an independent contractor. The evaluation showed that CLIPs members enhanced the quality of their collegial relationships as well as relationships with students, increased their knowledge and skills related to inquiry practices and evidence-based decision making, and diversified their strategies to influence student learning as a result of their involvement (Parsons, 2009).

University of British Columbia Medical Education Program

The Faculty of Medicine at UBC, building upon the experiences at Bakersfield College, launched a CLIPs initiative in its Medical Education Program in 2010. The program, which includes both undergraduate and postgraduate training, has 1,136 students, 1,335 residents, 677 full-time faculty, and 6,059 clinical faculty.

The 4-year Undergraduate Medical Degree (MD) program[3] is composed of four geographically distinct sites across the province. The distributed program aims to increase the number of rural and aboriginal students in medical careers, while allowing students to complete their training in rural and underserved communities, where, as studies suggest, they are more likely to return to practice following training. Student enrollment in the undergraduate program increased from 200 in 2004 to 288 in 2014. The program is accredited by the Committee on Accreditation of Canadian Medical Schools and the Liaison Committee on Medical Education in the United States. When students complete their undergraduate training they enter postgraduate (residency) training.

The postgraduate program trains residents in family medicine, together with 69 specialty and subspecialty training programs recognized by the Royal College of Physicians and Surgeons of Canada and the College of Family Physicians of Canada. Enrollment grew from 265 to 328 between 2010 and 2014. The duration of training varies from 2 years for family medicine to 4 to 7 years for other specialties and subspecialties.

The Evaluation Studies Unit (ESU), established in 2004, is responsible for evaluation of undergraduate and postgraduate medical education. The unit established a CLIPs program in 2010 in response to their lack of capacity to conduct all evaluations requested and as part of their efforts to build evaluation capacity within the Faculty of Medicine, as stated in their mandate. Between 2010 and 2014, 49 individuals participated in CLIPs (86% faculty), and there was a total of 23 groups. All but five groups com-

---

[3] In British Columbia, students admitted to medical school must have 90 undergraduate credits in English, biology, chemistry, etc. Most students have a bachelor's degree. It takes 4 additional years of undergraduate training to receive a medical degree. At the postgraduate level, medical residency training is directed through the university and requires from 2 to 7 years, depending on the area of specialty.

pleted their projects, with lack of time being the most common barrier to completion.

The topics of inquiry that faculty identified as being of interest to them addressed a range of areas, including the quality of tutor training for problem-based learning, clinical skills in the musculoskeletal courses, use of library resources, enhancing interprofessional practice, and curriculum restructuring in a variety of clinical and nonclinical areas.

In 2015, an evaluation of the CLIPs program was conducted by an external evaluator using a qualitative approach that addressed the following questions: (a) were the expectations and intended outcomes achieved, (b) did the program build evaluation capacity, and (c) what factors influenced implementation, delivery, and utilization? The evaluation findings suggested that the program delivered on a number of evaluation capacity-building outcomes at the participant, program, evaluation unit, and organizational levels.

Contrasting the Two Settings

The two higher education settings differed in their impetus for starting the CLIPs process. At Bakersfield College, CLIPs were established to respond to the pressure to meet new accreditation standards, whereas at UBC, it was to handle the demand on the evaluation unit to conduct evaluations. The two sites also differed in their existing structures to address accountability and evaluation. Bakersfield had an institutional research office that gathered and reported a considerable amount of data but did not conduct evaluations. The UBC Medical Education Program had an internal evaluation unit with five evaluators and supporting staff responsible for evaluation of the program where CLIPs were implemented. Both sites underwent an evaluation of their CLIPs program. The findings from these evaluations are reflected in this chapter and combined with the observations and reflections of the authors.

Designs for Two CLIPs Approaches

At Bakersfield College, three annual meetings supported the individual CLIPs and an overarching structure linked to the college's institutional effectiveness committee and the assessment committee. The assessment committee focused on student learning outcomes assessment. The CLIPs guide (supported by the CLIPs external coach during the period of NSF funding) was a faculty member who was also a member of the assessment committee. The guide organized three meetings annually. The assessment committee received applications on an annual basis from faculty and staff who wished to form a CLIP.

In the second example, the CLIPs process was operated through the Faculty of Medicine's ESU. "CLIPs" was renamed "E-CLIPs" (Evaluation

Communities of Learning, Inquiry, and Practice) because there was another national medical initiative using the CLIP acronym. A call for proposals was circulated once per year in the fall (a simple one-page form). An oversight committee, chaired by ESU's associate director (who also served as the CLIPs guide), was responsible for reviewing and selecting proposals, promoting the initiative, and providing strategic direction that linked to the overall goals of the institution. ESU evaluators were assigned to each group and served as a primary resource. Similar to the Bakersfield groups, at UBC, each group had an E-CLIPs leader (usually a faculty member) who was responsible for leading the group and the guide organized three meetings annually.

Both settings offered groups a small amount of funding (up to $1,000) to support groups in addressing their evaluation questions. The online training modules used in the Bakersfield College example were modified for relevance to the UBC setting. In both examples, the CLIPs groups most frequently collected data through questionnaires, focus groups, and interviews involving students, faculty, and others.

A Dialogue About CLIPs Guiding Principles

The preceding section describes the use of CLIPs/E-CLIPs in two postsecondary education settings to illustrate variation on how CLIPs were tailored to the settings. Based on these (and related) experiences, this section presents guiding principles in the form of a dialogue among Beverly (CLIP external coach for Bakersfield College), Chris (director of the UBC Unit responsible for E-CLIPs), Derek (UBC E-CLIPs guide), and Kylie (external evaluator contracted by UBC). We recommend the principles be used to establish CLIPs in any organization where professionals are engaging in evaluative activities but for whom evaluation is not their primary responsibility. We also encourage attention to the principles for establishing communities of practice in general as provided by Wenger and colleagues (2002).

The first version of the guiding principles emerged from the original work at Bakersfield College after the second round of CLIPs. A set of guiding principles was drafted based on the external evaluation from the first year and the experiences of the CLIPs coach. During the midyear meeting of CLIPs, participants reviewed draft guiding principles and provided examples of what they had done that illustrated the principles. Later, the CLIP guide, coach, and the evaluators adjusted the wording to better reflect what participants said about their situation. Over subsequent years and in working with other groups, and the variation used at UBC, we have identified a set of guiding principles for implementing CLIPs. These key principles should be considered when implementing CLIPs, whether in a postsecondary or another level of education, or a different sector (e.g., health, social programs, business, government, and nonprofit).

NEW DIRECTIONS FOR EVALUATION • DOI: 10.1002/ev

1. Ensure that CLIPs Ask Questions About Their Own Work that Matter to Them

Beverly: This principle was at the heart of conceptualizing the CLIPs process when we submitted the proposal to NSF for funding. So much evaluation is about someone else defining the questions and someone else carrying out an evaluation. The idea here was for faculty and staff to gather around a question that really mattered to them and one they wanted to investigate in their own way. By the end of the year, the CLIPs were expected to share something about what they learned; however, what they shared was up to them. In so doing, they needed to think about what was important to those they were communicating with and what they were willing to share with others. Some shared the results, say, of a survey they had done with students, whereas others shared the process they used and the benefits and challenges of collaborating with colleagues.

Chris: This principle also represents the heart of our E-CLIPS program, in fact it was the very reason we were drawn to the approach. We had been in operation as an internal evaluation unit for about 5 years and received many requests for evaluations that we couldn't fulfill. There were complaints that we weren't addressing many of the more basic questions that faculty were interested in asking. For example, an individual faculty member might be trying an innovative approach to teaching course material and wanted more information about whether it was working or not. We knew that we couldn't do it all and we saw E-CLIPs as a way to both support faculty in building evaluation into their work and reduce the demand on the evaluation unit.

Kylie: As the independent consultant tasked with evaluating the E-CLIP's program, it became evident to me that the opportunity to investigate an issue they were passionate about substantially increased participants' engagement with the project. This flexibility emerged as a clear factor in the success of E-CLIPs.

2. Foster a Safe, Hospitable, and Flexible Environment for Inquiry

Beverly: We used this principle in a number of ways. Creating a safe environment began with CLIPs selecting their own question and the colleagues with whom they would work. A hospitable environment was exemplified by the setting we created for joint meetings. We chose the most comfortable room available on campus and sometimes met in the recreation room at a nearby condominium complex that was within walking distance of the campus. We had food at the meetings. We set up the agenda so that participants from different departments on campus had a chance to meet and work with one another. Faculty were very eager to interact with one another around instructional issues.

Perhaps the most important aspect of having a flexible environment was how the CLIPs designed and carried out their work. Each CLIP presented an initial proposal to the Assessment Committee of its inquiry question(s) and how the members thought they might carry out their inquiry. We encouraged them to remain open to adjusting it as they got underway. At the first meeting, they developed their specific inquiry plan with timelines and assigned responsibilities, adjusting it to ensure they felt comfortable to actually carry it out within the time and resources they had. We kept encouraging them to cut it back and find the most important questions and processes that would give them a sense of success in completing the work. At the midyear meeting, they reflected carefully on what had been working so far. If they had taken on too much, again we encouraged them to adjust so they would actually finish and accomplish something that was important to them. If the CLIPs process was to be sustained over the coming years, faculty had to feel excitement and satisfaction about what they had accomplished.

Chris: We sought to foster a safe and hospitable environment by asking people to form their own groups. We reasoned that a sense of self-determination would create a safe environment in which people felt empowered to learn. The evaluators assigned to each group were oriented to the program under study and instructed to provide technical assistance that was supportive yet enabling and tailored to a group's specific needs, based on where they were in the process. For example, rather than present a large number of resources at the beginning, evaluators carefully selected and introduced resources on an as-needed basis. The group meetings were all held in our program offices, and we did not budget for refreshments.

Our E-CLIPs groups also started with a call for proposals that was open to any kind of evaluation question. Groups came to us with ideas about how they thought they might carry out their studies. We encouraged them to stay open to adjusting their approach and provided ideas for them to consider as appropriate.

However, on a different level, flexibility is something that we definitely want to enhance in the future. We placed a 1-year time frame on all studies and we had only one "call for proposals" in the fall. We learned that some groups justifiably needed more time to complete their work, and the 1-year deadline placed undue pressure on groups, which took away from the positive aspects of the experience. The once per year "call for proposals" was also a deterrent to some because it simply didn't fit the spontaneous emergence of opportunities and was out of sync with some aspects of the program.

Derek: As the E-CLIP's guide, my principal aim was to ensure that each group felt guided and supported through all phases of their evaluation project. However, I could see that the groups did face one significant challenge and that was finding the time for their projects. Group members told me that the time required to complete all of the necessary tasks for their study was often overwhelming in the midst of all their other responsibilities. As a result, there were several projects that were originally approved that never got off the ground or had to withdraw. In the future, we plan

NEW DIRECTIONS FOR EVALUATION • DOI: 10.1002/ev

to incorporate more structured activities and one-to-one coaching upfront before proposals are submitted. I think it will help them to break up the process into more doable chunks and create a feasible timeline.

3. Create Authentic, Open-Minded Dialogue that Reflects Diverse Perspectives

Beverly: The beauty of having CLIPs from a variety of departments was the diversity of perspectives that enriched the conversations during the three meetings of all the CLIPs each year. It also helped CLIP members see the bigger picture of the college as a whole. Bakersfield College administrators and faculty leaders were eager to initiate the CLIPs process on campus because it was a way to creatively engage faculty in responding to the accreditation push for more explicit student learning outcomes for all courses and for collegewide assessment of learning outcomes. It offered faculty a way to engage with their colleagues driven by their own internal motivation. The institutional effectiveness committee and assessment committee (both of which had CLIPs members) extended the norms and orientation of the CLIPs into these campuswide conversations. Seeing how these expectations regarding student learning outcomes played out in different departments and how they helped promote student learning was important. And it was grounded in actual data from students about their points of view about whatever the CLIPs was investigating. For example, hearing actual stories from students through surveys and focus groups about how, when, and where they studied opened the eyes of the faculty to the challenging lives of their students. Students' descriptions of working full time in addition to going to school, raising several children, living in a small apartment with multiple generations, having no quiet place at home to study, and spending considerable time on the bus to get to campus helped faculty see that the lives of their students were often much more complex than their own.

Chris: The opportunity for open dialogue about evaluation between the group and their evaluator has been a key element for group success. The very act of creating the time for groups to meet created a "space for reflection" in a normally hectic schedule. We noted two key areas of dialogue that occurred within the groups: First, critical dialogue occurred about the program component they were studying. They asked questions such as, "How do we describe what we are evaluating? What kind of change or improvement do we seek? How does this change fit within the larger organization?" The groups spent quite a bit of time discussing these questions. The second area related to framing appropriate evaluation questions, including what questions they wanted to answer, what was important to know, and what was a realistic scope given the limits of time.

Our E-CLIPs have been focused on a single academic program, and groups have not necessarily reflected diversity outside this area or across departments within the program; however, moving forward, we will try to encourage greater diversity of faculty and staff. It makes sense to me that extending the dialogue even further to include students would be useful.

Derek: E-CLIPs groups typically sought to quickly dive in and focus their first discussions on the details of the evaluation, only to realize that a critical first step in the process was to arrive at a consensus on the program component under study. These discussions promoted reflection and a critical appraisal of what they were doing. And given that faculty, staff, and learners often composed the E-CLIPs groups, a diversity of perspectives was represented in the dialogue.

4. Structure the CLIPs Process to Generate Sustained, Renewing, Inquiry-Based Practice

Beverly: This principle was fundamental to the CLIPs process in the community college setting. A core reason for setting up the process was to build inquiry into the ongoing life and practice of how faculty carried out their regular work. We wanted collaborative and systematic evaluative inquiry to become a regular process of how faculty thought and worked. We wanted the findings from a CLIP inquiry to provide insights that would convince the participants that activities such as gathering information from students about their reactions to a certain instructional practice was worthwhile. We wanted them to see what it meant to create a safe, hospitable environment for students to give feedback. The direct and personal experiences of participating in a CLIP in a flexible way were all part of building sustainability into the process. I was excited to see how the process took hold at Bakersfield College and continued for several years after the grant was over. Although it has ended, the value of it was sustained among many of the faculty in terms of their developing a greater valuing of evaluative inquiry about their own work.

Chris: We wanted to promote evaluative thinking and create a deeper understanding of the evaluation process and its value. Although we were successfully embedding evaluation into the higher level of the organizational structure and governance, we wanted to grow a culture of evaluation that permeated every level of the organization and didn't focus exclusively on the staff of our evaluation unit as the only people asking questions and conducting evaluations. We've seen some very positive and sustained results from the E-CLIPs experience. For example, participants have told us that they learned a lot about evaluation by doing it, and some went on to independently conduct additional evaluations on their own. We also have some new evaluation champions who are now engaging more actively in discussions about evaluation. We've also found that E-CLIPs assisted our evaluation unit in developing new and stronger relationships with stakeholders. An E-CLIPs model is becoming part of the way we do business.

NEW DIRECTIONS FOR EVALUATION • DOI: 10.1002/ev

To strengthen our approach, we want to engage more staff as E-CLIPs team leaders and members; to date the majority of participants have been faculty. One of the recommendations from the E-CLIPs evaluation was to engage students in participating in groups and in initiating studies. We are exploring the feasibility of expanding to allow students to initiate their own projects. It might be more than our internal evaluation unit can handle, but we might be able to engage some of our E-CLIPs alumni faculty in sponsoring students. All in all, E-CLIPs have been a win–win situation in terms of reinforcing inquiry-based practice.

Kylie: Although E-CLIPs were made available to both faculty and staff, 12 of the 14 groups were initiated and led by faculty members. In fact, the majority of participants were faculty. It is interesting to note that the evaluators assigned to each group observed that groups with a combination of both faculty and staff had a greater chance of reaching completion. Challenges with maintaining momentum were commonly reported. Moving forward, recommendations to address this include limiting project scope, encouraging a mix of faculty and staff E-CLIPs members, holding biannual opportunities for communication across groups, conducting mandatory monthly check-ins with the assigned evaluator, and screening groups for capacity at the preproposal stage.

5. Provide Participants with Tailored Evaluation Coaching Specific to Their Needs

Beverly: When we started the process in Bakersfield, I served as the evaluation coach for the CLIPs. I was from an outside evaluation and research organization that had received the funding to test this process. I had worked out a partnership relationship with the college to get the pilot study underway. I was serving as the evaluation coach to help get the work off the ground and to work closely with the faculty member from the assessment committee who would serve as the CLIPs guide over several years. She had basic knowledge about learning outcomes assessment and evaluation. We worked together in setting up the application process and planning and facilitating the joint CLIP meetings. We also intentionally connected the CLIPs process with the college's focus on student learning and assessment. This included arranging opportunities for faculty to share the results of their inquiries at collegewide faculty events, through newsletters, and by incorporating information about CLIPs inquiries in accreditation reports.

Over time, members of the assessment and institutional effectiveness committees provided coaching. Also, a number of the faculty involved in the CLIPs had expertise in quantitative data analysis. They were willing to help other CLIPs in setting up their analyses. Occasionally, a student played a role in providing expertise, such as in data analysis. Chris, you had a stronger model for ongoing evaluation coaching. I hope other

NEW DIRECTIONS FOR EVALUATION • DOI: 10.1002/ev

organizations can work out a design more like yours or come up with a way to maintain some support from an external coach.

Chris: One size doesn't fit all—we had to stay flexible. Each group was different and the evaluator working with them had to be able to determine what was needed when. Each of the E-CLIP teams received one-on-one technical assistance from an evaluation specialist from our internal unit and a variety of resources that addressed their specific needs. The evaluators met with their groups throughout the project. Our experience has been that evaluators are a key factor in determining the program's success. Stakeholders have been most appreciative of their expertise and especially liked having a single point of contact for evaluation assistance. Because our evaluators have been so central to the process, we will be focusing more time on orienting them to their roles and incorporating more of a coaching model (rather than an expert consultation model).

Kylie: During the evaluation of E-CLIPs, group leaders told me how much they appreciated having the one-to-one support and a single point of contact for evaluation information. Recall that these were extremely busy professionals with little extra time to read additional manuals or resources for evaluation. Their feedback on the support they received from their evaluator was overwhelmingly and universally positive. It seems there is no substitute for a knowledgeable voice at the other end of the phone or email.

Chris: We also want to expand this coaching to a "preproposal" phase in which the evaluator engages with E-CLIPs' applicants upfront before proposals are submitted. This would help us to address issues that will promote the success of the project. In general, we want to promote E-CLIPs as an empowering model. Given that E-CLIPs are only a small part of our work in the internal evaluation unit, I do worry about the amount of time evaluators will spend in a coaching role—this is something we'll have to continue to monitor.

Derek: Our internal evaluators have been very enthusiastic about embracing more of a coaching model going forward. We plan to conduct some internal training to enhance their skills in such areas as how to ask E-CLIPs participants empowering questions and how to foster buy-in, ownership of goals, and group commitment. I'm enthusiastic about this approach as well because I think it will translate into clearer role boundaries for our evaluators. I'm always cognizant of supporting them in balancing the many demands on their time.

6. Engender Simplicity and Empowerment

Beverly: We knew this process couldn't last if it was too complicated and if it felt imposed. Our focus on encouraging CLIPs members to ask questions that mattered to them and making it easy for them to form their own group and apply to be a CLIP was essential. The application was short. We encouraged them to develop just a rough idea of what they wanted to do, not a perfectly worked out plan. That made it easy for people to apply and gave them a sense of empowerment as they gathered for their first meeting and began working together, got support from the coach, and heard one another's plans. Being able to right then and there slim down their expectations and make it more realistic without going through a bureaucratic review was empowering. Their ability to make choices about what they disseminated to others was another example of empowerment and being treated as a professional.

Chris: In addition to working with an evaluator, each group was provided an evaluation guidebook and a variety of recommended resources according to their needs. We decided it was important to tailor the CLIPs evaluation guide to our specific context, so we reworked the original CLIPs materials. We kept things simple and direct, recognizing that our participants were not going to become evaluators but need to learn selected techniques that would help them address their specific evaluation goals within the medical education context.

The hard copy evaluation guides weren't used as much as we thought they would be and going forward we want to redesign them. The major issue was "time"—our participants felt overwhelmed with all the information. Our idea is to shrink the resources down to the absolute minimum by providing things like one-page tip sheets, checklists, and very brief instructional videos. As the saying goes, "information is power" and providing participants material that is highly accessible, whether in written form or through the connection with an evaluator, we are empowering them to use evaluation to address questions that are meaningful to them.

Kylie: As the external evaluator, I was struck by the simplicity and effectiveness of the E-CLIPs model. Using relatively minimal inputs, E-CLIPs were able to successfully deliver on a number of evaluation capacity-building outcomes, including increased appreciation and knowledge of evaluation, increased independent evaluation activity, better quality evaluation, more internal evaluation champions, and the increased use of evidence for program improvement.

7. Build Connections Among the CLIPs and Between the CLIPs Process and the Organization's Overall Goals and Evaluation Plans and Rhythms of the Organization

Beverly: Building connections among the CLIPs and fitting with the overall goals and plans of the organization were central to our approach. We took a systemic approach to understanding the CLIPs in the context of the larger rhythms, patterns, and dynamics of the college. What are the norms? How do you work within those norms on one hand and start to adjust those norms on the other? In the case of Bakersfield College, the faculty and administrators on the assessment and institutional effectiveness committees knew how delicate the balance was between building faculty

NEW DIRECTIONS FOR EVALUATION • DOI: 10.1002/ev

support for attention to student learning outcomes and assessment on one hand and faculty sensitivity to administrative mandates on the other. The CLIPs process—which built on faculty members' choice of whether and when to participate, what the focus of their inquiry would be, who they would work with, and what they would share with whom about the results of their inquiries—kept the focus on student learning and faculty decision making rather than administrative mandates.

Chris: To date, the questions addressed by E-CLIPs groups have been quite diverse, and there was little focus on cross-talk among projects in the beginning, which, I now think, really limited the kind of synergism that could nurture capacity building across the organization. We have been focusing on a systems perspective in our work and encouraging our stakeholders to use evaluation in a way that considers how the various elements of the curriculum are linked. We have found that a midyear project status meeting and an end of year meeting in which groups share their results with one another have been very successful in building knowledge and enthusiasm about both evaluation and the topics studied, as well as the commonalities and links between various parts of the system.

In order for this program to remain sustainable, we'll need E-CLIPs to reflect the overall rhythms of the organization such as changes in pedagogy, special teaching initiatives, and accreditation site visits. To really get the most out of it, I think we'll need to be able to make changes from year to year according to the needs of the organization—and still maintain the vision of empowerment and the goal of promoting a culture of evaluation. For example, we've considered focusing our E-CLIPs program solely on the first year of our undergraduate curriculum, which has just undergone a major redesign. Our Evaluation Studies Unit is, of course, conducting an evaluation of the new curriculum, but we simply don't have the capacity to address many of the interesting questions that are arising from faculty and staff who are interested to learn about these changes.

Summary and Conclusion

In this chapter, we have illustrated a process for building evaluation capacity among professionals within an organization by describing two different applications of the CLIPs model in postsecondary institutions. We have provided concrete examples of the approach we used as well as seven guiding principles that can be used by those in other institutional settings. We encourage thoughtful reflection on your own situation and wise adaptation of these examples and principles. We welcome the opportunity to connect with you individually.

References

Parsons, B. (2009). Evaluative inquiry for complex times. *OD Practitioner. 41*, 44–49.

Preskill, H. (2014). Now for the hard stuff: Next steps in ECB research and practice. *American Journal of Evaluation. 35*(1), 116–119.
Wenger, E., McDermott, R., & Snyder, W. (2002). *Cultivating communities of practice.* Boston: Harvard Business School Press.
Wenger, E., & Snyder, W. (2000). Communities of practice: The organizational frontier. *Harvard Business Review. 78*(1), 139–145.

BEVERLY L. PARSONS *is the executive director of InSites, a nonprofit evaluation, research, and planning organization.*

CHRIS Y. LOVATO *(formerly the director of the Evaluation Studies Unit) is a professor in the School of Population & Public Health, University of British Columbia.*

KYLIE HUTCHINSON *is a principal consultant with Community Solutions, a program planning and evaluation consulting firm.*

DEREK WILSON *(formerly associate director) is the director of the Evaluation Studies Unit, University of British Columbia, Faculty of Medicine.*

NEW DIRECTIONS FOR EVALUATION • DOI: 10.1002/ev

Stevenson, J F., Hicks, S J., & Hubbard, A. (2016). Evaluating a general education program in transition In W. H. Rickards, & M. Stitt-Bergh (Eds.), *Evaluating student learning in higher education: Beyond the public rhetoric. New Directions for Evaluation, 151,* 37–51.

3

Evaluating a General Education Program in Transition

John F. Stevenson, Sandy Jean Hicks, Anne Hubbard

Abstract

This reflective case study uses one public university example to explore the role of student learning outcomes assessment in the improvement of general education programs. These programs are a universal feature of higher education in the United States, requiring learning experiences for all students at an institution— but with little likely commitment from the faculty. Our university's efforts to overcome faculty apathy and resistance, build a responsive assessment system, and direct it toward transformation of our program are instructive beyond the higher education context. We take a participatory, utilization-focused approach and reflect on what we have learned as it illuminates both the relevance of evaluation concepts to our work in assessment and the contributions from our context to the broader domains of evaluation conceptualization and practice. © 2016 Wiley Periodicals, Inc., and the American Evaluation Association.

Learning outcomes assessment is a form of program evaluation with its own special challenges and opportunities, but it is also a locus for valuable lessons for the broader field of evaluation. The authors have been engaged for several years with a particular example of these challenges and opportunities, directed at a uniquely important aspect of the higher education mission—institution-wide curricular requirements usually termed "general education." In U.S. higher education, students complete a set of "general education" requirements that are usually designed as foundational to degree program requirements and as preparation for a literate life in a modern, global society. We use our experience as a case study to reflect on an assessment process, unfolding over a decade and set in a public land-grant university, to examine the role evaluation can play in addressing the learning outcomes from such programs. As we demonstrate, this is notoriously contested territory for program evaluation, and even the definition given here can provoke argument. Evaluators who venture onto this terrain do so at their peril.

This chapter brings to light tensions that exist in higher education settings: between accountability and improvement, administration and faculty, and varied disciplinary perspectives and allegiances. In our case, the program was undergoing a challenging change process for which the evaluators, functioning as reflective practitioners from within our faculty roles, tried valiantly to supply data for informed decision making while also responding to external requirements.

Although external accountability demands were the original impetus for learning outcomes assessment in colleges and universities, and for general education outcomes in particular, more recent aspirations call for internally directed assessment for improvement, shifting the focus to faculty engagement in a participatory, formative program improvement process. Building the motivation and capacity of university faculty to take primary responsibility for defining, measuring, and learning from their program's learning objectives is an ongoing process, particularly complicated for the context of general education program assessment. As we illustrate, the role of stakeholders' diverse epistemological traditions and contested values is reflected in negotiated choices for outcome measurement, definitions of program boundaries, and interactions between data and political priorities in program change.

Context

It is useful to understand context in terms of the program, the institution, and the local stakeholders.

General Education Program Context

Why is general education a special context for evaluation in higher education? For one thing, growing external demands for accountability have been particularly intense for the accomplishment of broad learning outcomes usually linked to general education (Banta, Jones, & Black, 2009; Kanter, Gamson, & London, 1997). These learning outcomes traditionally focused on knowledge from distinct disciplinary traditions (i.e., the humanities, natural sciences, and social sciences). More recent emphases include critical thinking, information literacy, quantitative reasoning, and written and oral communication. They may also include respect for diversity,

NEW DIRECTIONS FOR EVALUATION • DOI: 10.1002/ev

teamwork, ethics, civic engagement, and lifelong learning. To show, they take external accountability seriously, many schools are now satisfying the need for summative evaluation by opting for commercially designed objective measures for institution-wide outcomes (about 40% in a national survey reported by Kuh & Ewell in 2010). As with summative approaches across the wider field of evaluation, this focus on external accountability has the appearance of being more "objective" but may lead to resistance rather than improvement.

The formative path is not an easy alternative. As university administrators continue to focus on assessment's role in meeting external demands, faculty suspect that summative use will be made of any assessment results they report (Banta & Blaich, 2010), and evidence of genuine internal use has been slow to materialize (Blaich & Wise, 2011). Allen (2006) elaborates on some additional challenges specific to formative assessment of general education. These include the primary allegiance of faculty to their individual disciplines, the difficulties in coordinating assessment planning and implementation across a wide array of departments and programs in a "loosely coupled" organization (Weick, 1976), and the extensive use of part-time instructors, who have little time for university service obligations. Furman (2013) makes the issue of the tension between external accountability using standardized measures and faculty engagement and empowerment for formative assessment the centerpiece of her article. She points to the difficulties of getting faculty to agree on the purpose of general education requirements. As the one place in the curriculum that explicitly reflects institution-wide commitments to particular learning goals for students, these requirements are fraught with internal arguments for alternative value-based outcome agendas: utilitarian competence training vs. political/ideological concerns for multicultural, global, and citizenship preparation vs. less tangible mind-opening and lifelong-learning aspirations. That these arguments also have direct resource allocation implications both within the institution and beyond it (at least in public higher education institutions) only intensifies the disputes. Furman (2013) also notes the lack of accountability for general education. Involving the faculty in the assessment of the program is essential, and yet "this is precisely the issue that proves problematic" (p. 134)—unlike discipline-based degree programs, the general education program is usually an orphan, with no clear organizational home and no loyal faculty community.

Institutional Context

The setting for our case study is a midsized public university (15,660 students in 2014–2015), the land-grant institution for our state, with eight degree-granting colleges. For many years, the general education requirements followed a "loosely constrained menu of course choices" model as described by Furman (2013, p. 132). Two efforts to revise the general education program to include current ideas about pedagogy, content, interdisciplinarity, and experiential learning failed in the 1990s. However, in 2005, a plan to integrate skills within the existing structure led to infusion of more emphasis on competencies such as writing, quantitative reasoning, oral communication, and information literacy into content courses.

At about the same time, the external emphasis on learning outcomes assessment intensified. As a public institution, we needed to respond to the higher education governing board in our state, which had recognized the growing pressure from our regional accrediting agency. Institution-wide outcomes such as writing and critical thinking were explicitly featured in their concern. Within a year, a special committee began looking at what students thought about their general education courses, and what the best ways to frame learning outcome objectives for our program would be. That is where our case narrative begins.

Local Stakeholders

Faculty from departments that offer general education courses and those that do not (but whose students take them) represent important stakeholder groups. Our own involvement has been from the faculty perspective, with our prior knowledge of assessment and program evaluation drawing us in as we saw the growing opportunity to bring our skills and values to the problem of general education reform with assessment a driving force. We have served in leadership roles on relevant committees and pressed for self-directed, data-oriented ways of improving the general education experience of our students. We have worked collaboratively with provosts, deans, and directors of institution-wide assessment (the administrative perspective), as well as colleagues from many academic departments, serving on our general education committee, a subcommittee for assessment of general education (SAGE), and a task force focused on development of innovative courses for first-year students that was intended to start a path toward a new general education program. Policy making for general education moves from the general education committee to our faculty senate (both with modest student representation) and at that level also requires the provost's approval. All three of us have served on the university's general education committee, and two of us have chaired it. One of us has served as president of the faculty senate. The three of us have had relatively central responsibility for work on general education assessment planning and implementation, as well as for capacity building with our colleagues. The university's assessment office and its evolving core staff represent another major stakeholder. Formed in response to the external pressure, they became the source of much of the creative energy, importation of expertise to inform the effort and strategically directed support of faculty like us. The director of that office was instrumental in recruiting us to work on

NEW DIRECTIONS FOR EVALUATION • DOI: 10.1002/ev

general education outcomes assessment, and as a result, we have been involved collaboratively with that office from the beginning of the process described here.

Case Study Narrative

Our case narrative incorporates illustrative methods, data, and the give and take of developmental processes, both formal and informal.

Developing Learning Outcomes for the Program

In 2007, the newly appointed director of assessment identified faculty with political credibility and evaluation and/or assessment expertise from across the institution . We were among that group. This select committee, the first incarnation of SAGE, spent a summer defining the learning outcomes of the recently revised program, retrofitting them as the external demands became unmistakable. What emerged was strikingly similar to the Bloom, Engelhart, Furst, Hill, and Krathwohl (1956) taxonomy of cognitive objectives, applied to each core knowledge area of our requirements (i.e., social sciences, natural sciences, arts and literature, and humanities) and incorporating real-world problems as part of the learning experiences (and hence contexts for assessment) in each of those domains. The outcomes were stated broadly—for example, "Ability to ask questions appropriate to the modes of inquiry in the fine arts and literature in relevant academic and nonacademic contexts."

First Effort at Data Collection

To begin applying those outcome objectives, the select committee devised a stratified random sample of all general education courses offered in the fall of 2007 and collected data (student surveys and a sample of student work) from each course in the sample. Aware of a skeptical faculty view that most general education courses were primarily oriented toward the memorization of facts rather than higher-order learning, the committee hoped to clarify the reality of actual learning experiences as seen by students and as demonstrated in faculty assignments. In evaluation terms, the intent was to determine the extent to which the newly defined outcomes could be linked to the practices in the existing program. This in turn could inform the development of rubrics (categorical schemas for evaluating qualitative work) for the outcomes, clarify the workload implications of implementing assessment in general education courses, and identify promising pedagogical practices for future program improvement initiatives. All of those steps were seen as precursors to full-blown assessment of the current program that would hold it accountable to the newly devised outcomes. In the summer of 2008, the director of assessment recruited the three of us to form a subcommittee of SAGE to employ the sample of assignments and student work to take on those tasks. From the beginning, the intention of SAGE and our summer task group was to use rubric-based judgments of actual student work on meaningful projects and assignments to define program success as opposed to a commercially designed, externally normed, instrument.

The findings were generally reassuring and in some ways more positive than the committee had anticipated. The preponderance of all classified assignments in core knowledge domains (82%) called for more than rote memorization and over half called for one or more levels of "analysis." Although few called for students to generate their own original hypotheses or major questions, 23% did call for active collection of data (e.g., laboratory investigation, review of relevant published literature, and systematic qualitative observation). Many (73%) called for students to recognize which concepts could be used to answer a question or solve a problem, and most of those also called for the student to follow through on applying the concepts to arrive at a solution. We modified one outcome, *Analysis*, by dividing it into three subcategories in order to better represent the types of assignment choices we found in our data. The sample did not adequately represent the literature and fine arts areas, and we anticipated possible barriers to future participation of these fields in general education.

Based on this experience, SAGE began plotting next steps toward ongoing measurement of general education outcomes. We reached out to faculty who taught general education courses across the disciplines to help us refine the rubrics by pilot testing them with assignments in their courses. Although the new outcomes were formally approved, there was virtually no effort to actively integrate them into the program. SAGE recognized that fundamental issue but chose to move slowly, expecting broader implementation with one or more of the core knowledge areas to become more possible after the piloting process. The membership of SAGE included members of the policy-making general education committee, but there was very little effort to make a direct connection, as the typical role of that committee was simply to approve course proposals for new general education courses.

Beginning of Transition: A New Provost

The arrival of a new provost with openly avowed intentions to modernize and revitalize general education was seen by faculty across the institution as an opportunity for the "better" program they dreamed of (although the dreams were quite varied, reflecting the different values of faculty subcultures). The provost also made it clear that he was uninterested in using the assessment process that was under way to inform development of an innovative new program. Unfortunately, many faculty treated this as a reason to forego any further evaluation of the existing program. Stymied, the assessment committee searched for new ways to comply with external accountability requirements and make data-driven contributions to internal conversations about possible changes in the program. The assessment office leadership pressed for application of widely accepted rubrics for "skills"-oriented outcomes such as writing, oral communication, and information literacy, but SAGE members were unsure how to justify the application of learning outcomes that had never been approved by the faculty.

The "Grand Challenge" First-Year Seminar Innovation

A promising target for renewed engagement in program assessment presented itself through the provost-sponsored set of special "global challenge" topical courses called Grand Challenge (GCH) for first-year students. The assumption, based on current trends in higher education (Umback & Wawrzynski, 2005), was that having senior faculty instructors who are knowledgeable and enthusiastic about their topic area would in turn engage beginning college students more effectively in their education.

Although assessment was not a priority for this initiative, SAGE effectively argued for the inclusion of outcome assessment in order to continue to meet external reporting requirements and to determine the effectiveness of GCH courses. The assessment office was eager to help and contributed expertise all along the way. Consequently, a series of assessment methods were developed and employed, with data fed back periodically to important faculty bodies. Faculty involved in the first iteration of the GCH courses participated in SAGE-led focus groups in November 2010 to discuss core features of the initiative. The responses were recorded and coded. Faculty identified several major problems: the students' "readiness" in regards to skill sets necessary to engage in the expected level of work; the need to provide students with a high degree of structure; the interdisciplinary design of the program, which paired GCH courses with either a writing or communication course; and finally, restriction of enrollment to first-semester freshmen.

Students' opinions were also sought. SAGE designed a 10-question Likert-scale survey with input from the GCH task force. The survey was distributed in GCH seminar classes at the same time as the course evaluations at the end of the fall 2010 semester. Results suggested that overall students were positive about their GCH experience. Feeling more connected to other students, accessibility and supportiveness of faculty, and focus on problems facing the world were all highly rated. However, less than half felt the interdisciplinary structure of the GCH experience was working as intended.

This information was combined with faculty focus group input by the GCH task force to inform the redesign of the program structure and refine instructor training and support for the second year. Selected first-year GCH faculty who continued in the second year served as mentors to new GCH faculty. Redesigned workshops based on the faculty and student data were offered in the spring of 2011 and fall of 2012. Using student assignment data from the first year of GCH, workshops focused on the links between learning outcomes and pedagogy were substantially enhanced, with inclusion of peer illustrations of how scaffolded assignments could improve learning and accomplish multiple outcomes. Recognizing the daunting logistics and failure to achieve intended ends, the interdisciplinary pairing of GCH seminars with skills courses was eliminated. Similar rounds of data collection proceeded in two subsequent fall semesters.

The SAGEs learned a great deal: the most productive effects were "process-use" effects, with faculty in focus groups discovering their shared experiences, exploring ways of engaging students with appropriate challenges, and debating whether learning outcomes made any real difference. To some extent, the SAGE aspiration to establish a learning community of faculty more knowledgeable about outcomes and assessment for general education was accomplished. Ironically, one result was that various key faculty stakeholders recognized the logistical difficulty of extending the assessment process to the entire general education program.

General Education Committee Engagement with Transition

Concurrently, and in response to the provost's urging along with pressure from some quarters of the faculty, the general education committee began to converge on a new set of learning outcomes and a revised structure of course requirements to achieve them. Committee research identified the outcomes promoted by the Association of American Colleges and Universities (AAC&U) as a valuable model to adapt for local conditions. The capacity of faculty involved with general education policy and assessment had increased substantially, in part through the experience with GCH implementation and assessment. Building on the increased capacity and the rapidly spreading recognition that accreditation requirements mandated action, the general education committee applied itself to a real effort at transformation to an outcomes-driven program. New attention to assessment via rubric-development retreats, subsequent outcome-focused committees, a revised outcome-driven course proposal form, model assignments, recommendations for instructor training, and surfacing of unresolved issues all showed the benefits of external accreditation pressure moving us toward internal sense-making for improved pedagogy and curriculum.

Status of the Transition and the Central Role of Assessment

Recognizing workload demands associated with faculty-led evaluation, faculty began to focus on outcomes for which there was a constituency and an adaptable measurement method usable by academic departments as well as for general education assessment. With the behind-the-scenes guidance of our assessment office that provided minigrants and information about a set of AAC&U rubrics termed Valid Assessment of Learning in Undergraduate Education (VALUE) being used by other institutions assessing learning outcomes (Sullivan, 2015). These rubrics were identified as models for our rubric development. In 2011, the assessment office used its own resources to support a model for the rubric adaptation process. The effort was spearheaded by the library faculty; those teaching GCH courses and those working on assessment of general education began developing and pilot testing a rubric for information literacy. Subsequently, changes were made based on the data received from that pilot, the rubric was revised, and then more data were collected.

In spring 2012, the faculty senate approved 11 proposed learning outcomes as an organizing framework for the revised program. These outcomes encompassed three classes of outcomes—"knowledge" (similar to our original "core knowledge" outcomes), "responsibilities" (e.g., global competence), and "competencies" (e.g., mathematical and statistical). With leadership from SAGE and the assessment office, other learning outcome rubrics began to emerge following the path pioneered for information literacy.

Pressure from the university administration and the faculty senate leadership to bring a final structure to the faculty senate resulted in an increased pace in the development of the structure and assessment plan. The data collected from the GCH initiative had modest relevance for the proposed program, which requires a Grand-Challenge-themed course and includes a student learning outcome focused on interdisciplinary experiences. A proposed structure was promulgated in December 2013. Members of the general education committee and SAGE visited college, department, and student senate meetings to address questions about the structure and assessment of the revised program. The new program was approved in March 2014.

In the fall of 2014, SAGE formally recommended the use of the VALUE rubrics as a basis for operationalizing program outcomes, which was approved by the general education committee. Faculty leaders on the general education committee, supported by the expertise in the assessment office, grasped the importance of internal ownership of the outcomes and assessment process as essential to promote formative internal use and created cross-disciplinary committees to focus on assessment of each outcome. The committee-approved rubrics resulting from this process are now being used to define expectations for proposed courses and to guide faculty in revising and creating courses and assignments for the new program. The assessment office participated in the design of the workshops offered to help faculty find their way into the new outcome-based model for their courses. At the same time, the rubric revision process has become a battleground for concerns about whose outcomes matter and the associated resource

NEW DIRECTIONS FOR EVALUATION • DOI: 10.1002/ev

implications. The rubric developed by SAGE long ago in 2007–2008 to assess core knowledge outcomes is being used, with some modifications, in the new program. General education will be defined by its learning outcomes and every course will be designed to achieve one or more of those outcomes. Plans for technologically feasible sampling of rubric results in a multiyear cycle are in development, involving collaboration between SAGE and the assessment office.

Contributions of Evaluation Theory and Methods to Assessment

Although learning outcomes assessment began as a pedagogical concern, it has for many years been a form of program evaluation, and we perceive constructive influence in both directions. Evaluation influences include working toward utilization from the outset, developing the capacity for a "learning organization," and recognizing the role of the power and perspectives of multiple stakeholder groups in influencing evaluation processes and uses.

Utilization Focus

The long history of concern for the effectiveness of evaluation in producing real change is clearly relevant for the higher education assessment context. Johnson and her coauthors provide a compelling summary of the literature on utilization, arguing that "evaluation theory provides a framework for considering a broader model of possible uses of assessment evidence" (Johnson, Guetterman, & Thompson, 2014, p. 19). They demonstrate with an application of Kirkhart's (2000) multidimensional theory of influence to the general education assessment context, while also drawing on other evaluation luminaries such as Patton, Weiss, and Preskill and Torres who attend to utilization issues. Our own case example has aimed for direct instrumental application of assessment data to decision making, with modest success. Although we achieved some direct influence from assessing the GCH freshman seminar program, we did not initially recognize the weak connection between assessment planning and implementation, on the one hand, and the policy-making structure, on the other. We should have paid more attention to the advice of Kinnick (1985) on the importance of creating the necessary organizational structures to facilitate essential linkages between those who collect the evidence and those who will use it. Targeting intended users, as Patton (2008) advises, proved far from easy in so complex a decision process. Despite our limited instrumental effectiveness, we have seen conceptual use expand the understanding of the general education committee and many other concerned faculty as they come to see the value of certain kinds of pedagogies (e.g., scaffolded assignments addressing real-world problems) and the particular difficulties in challenging students to integrate learning from varied disciplines as well as the broader approach to learning that requires constant attention to clearly defined outcomes and feedback on their achievement.

We have attempted to be participatory and decision focused from the outset and shifted our assessment targets as the external political process called for new kinds of answers. Process use has been remarkably important in our work—asking a faculty committee or a group of instructors, across disciplines, to work together to define the intended learning outcomes for general education and how they will be accomplished is a dramatic intervention into the system. Communally creating rubrics to measure those outcomes is another, and using faculty focus groups to discuss how innovative first-year seminars were addressing learning outcomes is a third.

Stakeholder Conflict

A second powerful message from the evaluation field concerns the complex aspects of social program evaluation with multiple stakeholders. Most higher education institutions are not "top down" in their decision-making structure, and many stakeholders with high status, advanced degrees, and strong professional values and economic interests roil the process of transition to a new program, even as they contribute to it. The evaluation literature is replete with advice and methods for involving varied stakeholders. Mabry (2010) poses particular challenges from a postpositivist evaluator's perspective, suggesting that evaluators may be seen as "the hired lackeys of those who can afford to pay them" (Mabry, 2010, p. 93). We experienced that perspective first hand. Ideological differences among faculty themselves, along lines envisioned by evaluation theorists like Guba and Lincoln (2004), were also present from the outset. As Segerholm (2010) points out, even the basic questions of what purposes education serves and for whom are contested, so the views of faculty stakeholders will unsurprisingly clash in framing the role and structure of general education. Recognizing the likelihood of these rough waters, we attempted to build in opportunities for broad faculty participation from the first development of outcome statements through the definition of criteria for assessing them and the evolution of rubrics. Despite these efforts, the grounding of current assessment practice in a positivist social science assumptive framework, along with the sense of disempowerment of the humanities and fine arts disciplines (particularly in a more technically oriented land-grant university), inevitably led to continuing confrontation and resistance. In the end, it was a very close and contentious faculty vote that approved the revised general education program with its new learning outcomes. Long-standing tensions in the evaluation field are alive and well in the higher education assessment context, but at least we can anticipate and acknowledge them as we draw on the insights from evaluation experience.

How General Education Assessment Experience Can Inform Evaluation

Features of general education assessment can also shed new light on evaluation topics, including the special nature of a learning organization whose central purpose is learning; the assertiveness of diverse academic cultures with their varying epistemological and value traditions and proud expertise of their proponents; the value of "authentic" measures of desired outcomes; and the special role of an administration-directed assessment office that subtly guides from behind.

Value on Learning

The challenges and strategies for fitting a formative, improvement-oriented approach to general education learning outcomes assessment into the existing accountability-oriented structure has broader implications for other settings for evaluation. What does it take to get a "learning community" orientation into an organizational culture, and what can result from doing so? The university context provides a preexisting emphasis on learning as a central mission, and the development of faculty learning communities in which professional development is a peer-driven enterprise is a useful laboratory for similar evaluation circumstances in other professionally oriented organizations (Driscoll & Wood, 2007; Johnson et al., 2014; Pace, 1985). As advocated by Johnson et al. (2014), we have sought to build learning communities (Preskill & Torres, 2000) to make assessment meaningful and useful, particularly with the first-year seminar instructors but also with rubric development teams and the general education committee.

Home of the Paradigm Wars

The university context provides another special challenge relevant for program evaluation: many of those who deliver the program are expected to evaluate it but are trained to question the value of quantitative measurement and causal logic. More fundamentally, they are trained to view positivist social science methods as a tool of the enemy. Mabry's (2010) history of the evolution of paradigmatic conflict aptly illustrates the central role of academic discourses in shaping the ideological struggles in the evaluation field. At our institution several colleagues have asserted that learning outcomes assessment is an aspect of the "corporatization" of the university. The ability of faculty to articulate these views tenaciously and persuasively is well represented by articles by Brody (2013) and Buller (2013), both affiliated with the humanities. Buller (2013) points to the accountability culture in higher education and the distorting pressure to demonstrate return on investment; Brody (2013, p. 20) astutely notes, "Paradoxically, one of the primary goals of teaching the humanities in today's world should be to call into question this very notion of objectivity that so many want to use to evaluate even the humanities." With views so well entrenched and articulately presented, the general education assessment context calls for new learning about how to make evaluation meaningful. We believe our own case example illustrates some evolution in ways to accomplish evidence-informed change in the midst of an ongoing paradigm war among the stakeholders.

Measuring What Matters

The use of "authentic" student work brings assessment closer to the perspectives of participants and can improve utilization. Some institutions have banded together to preserve more "authentic" and internally useful ways of assessing learning (Multi-State Collaborative, n.d.), in an attempt to bridge the formative-summative divide. Developing measurement approaches that have external psychometric acceptability and norms, as well as internal credibility and relevance, reflects a tension familiar in many evaluation contexts. Our work on rubric development and identification of exemplary peer models illustrates how problems with the use of externally developed standardized tests to measure learning outcomes (Furman,2013) have generated useful alternative approaches to measurement with direct relevance for faculty functioning as internal decision makers for program improvement.

Leading from Behind

Skillful leading from behind by our internal assessment office offers a model for other similar organizations. Interventions include identifying potential leaders, providing resources, promoting internal use of findings, while simultaneously attending to those external accountability demands that are the reason for its existence. Strategically placed minigrants, summer faculty reimbursement, peer-led faculty development workshops, and ex-officio participation on committees all nurtured the assessment culture and its incorporation in general education.

Conclusions

The pace of program change in higher education often seems glacial. Constant turnover in committee and administrative leadership and membership necessitated constant readjustments on the part of evaluators, both on the faculty side and the professional assessment staff side. We were challenged by a diverse, contentious, and ever-changing group of stakeholders, and we learned more about their reasons for resistance as well as their dedication to students as we went along. Decisions sometimes ran far ahead of data. In this context, evaluators may need to devote themselves to an iterative process of continued education and engagement and an acceptance of the value of process and conceptual use of their work.

NEW DIRECTIONS FOR EVALUATION • DOI: 10.1002/ev

References

Allen, M. J. (2006). *Assessing general education programs*. San Francisco, CA: Jossey-Bass.

Banta, T. W., & Blaich, C. (2010). Closing the assessment loop. *Change: The Magazine of Higher Learning. 43*(1), 22–27.

Banta, T. W., Jones, E. A., & Black, K. E. (2009). *Designing effective assessment: Principles and profiles of good practice*. San Francisco, CA: Jossey-Bass.

Blaich, C., & Wise, K. (2011). *From gathering to using assessment results: Lessons from the Wabash National Study* (Occasional Paper #8). Champaign, IL: National Institute for Learning Outcomes Assessment.

Bloom, B. S., Engelhart, M. D., Furst, E. J., Hill, W. H., & Krathwohl, D. R. (1956). *Taxonomy of educational objectives: The classification of educational goals. Handbook 1: Cognitive domain*. New York, NY: Longman.

Brody, H. (2013). Evaluating the humanities. *Academe. 99*(1), 19–23.

Buller, J. L. (2013). Academic leadership 2.0. *Academe. 99*(3), 28–33.

Driscoll, A., & Wood, S. (2007). *Outcomes-based assessment for learner-centered education*. Sterling, VA: Stylus.

Furman, T. (2013). Assessment of general education. *Journal of General Education. 62*(2–3), 129–136.

Guba, E. G., & Lincoln, Y. S. (2004). Chapter 1. Competing paradigms in qualitative research. In S. N. Hesse-Biber & P. Leavy (Eds.), *Approaches to qualitative research: A reader on theory and practice*. New York, NY: Oxford Press.

Johnson, J. L., Guetterman, T., & Thompson, R. J. (2014). An integrated model of influence: Use of assessment data in higher education. *Research & Practice in Assessment. 9*, 18–30. Retrieved from http://www.rpajournal.com/

Kanter, S. L., Gamson, Z. F., & London, H. B. (1997). *Revitalizing general education in a time of scarcity*. Needham Heights, MA: Allyn & Bacon.

Kinnick, M. K. (1985). Increasing the use of student outcomes information. In P. T. Ewell (Ed.), *New Directions for Institutional Research: No. 47. Assessing educational outcomes* (pp. 62–78). San Francisco, CA: Jossey-Bass.

Kirkhart, K. (2000). Reconceptualizing evaluation use: An integrated theory of influence. In V. J. Caracelli & H. Preskill (Eds.), *New Directions for Evaluation: No. 88. The expanding scope of evaluation use* (pp. 5–24). San Francisco, CA: Jossey-Bass.

Kuh, G. D., & Ewell, P. T. (2010). The state of learning outcomes assessment in the United States. *Higher Education Management & Policy. 22*(1), 9–28.

Mabry, L. (2010). Critical social theory evaluation: Slaying the dragon. In M. Freeman (Ed.), *New Directions for Evaluation: No. 127. Critical social theory and evaluation practice* (pp. 83–98). San Francisco, CA: Jossey-Bass.

Multi-State Collaborative. (n.d.). Retrieved from http://www.sheeo.org/projects/msc-multi-state-collaborative-advance-learning-outcomes-assessment

Pace, C. R. (1985). Perspectives and problems in student outcomes research. In P.T. Ewell (Ed.), *New Directions for Institutional Research: No. 47. Assessing educational outcomes* (pp. 7–18). San Francisco, CA: Jossey-Bass.

Patton, M. Q. (2008). *Utilization-focused evaluation*. Thousand Oaks, CA: Sage Publications.

Preskill, H., & Torres, R. T. (2000). The learning dimension of evaluation use. In V. J. Caracelli & H. Preskill (Eds.), *New Directions for Evaluation: No. 88. The expanding scope of evaluation use* (pp. 25–37). San Francisco, CA: Jossey-Bass.

Segerholm, C. (2010). Examining outcomes-based educational evaluation through a critical theory lens. In M. Freeman (Ed.), *New Directions for Evaluation: No. 127. Critical social theory and evaluation practice* (pp. 59–69). San Francisco, CA: Jossey-Bass.

Sullivan, D. F. (2015). *The VALUE breakthrough: Getting the assessment of student learning in college right*. Washington, DC: Association of American Colleges & Universities.

NEW DIRECTIONS FOR EVALUATION • DOI: 10.1002/ev

Umback, P., & Wawrzynski, M. (2005). Faculty do matter: The role of college faculty in student learning and engagement. *Research in Higher Education. 46*(2), 153–184.

Weick, K. E. (1976). Educational organizations as loosely coupled systems. *Administrative Science Quarterly. 21*(1), 1–19.

JOHN F. STEVENSON *is a professor emeritus of psychology at the University of Rhode Island.*

SANDY JEAN HICKS *is an associate professor in the School of Education at the University of Rhode Island.*

ANNE HUBBARD *is an assistant professor and the coordinator of the Bachelor of Interdisciplinary Studies at the University of Rhode Island.*

NEW DIRECTIONS FOR EVALUATION • DOI: 10.1002/ev

Rickards, W H., Abromeit, J., Mentkowski, M., & Mernitz, H. (2016). Engaging faculty in
an evaluative conversation. In W. H. Rickards & M. Stitt-Bergh (Eds.), *Evaluating student
learning in higher education: Beyond the public rhetoric. New Directions for Evaluation, 151,*
53–68.

4

Engaging Faculty in an Evaluative Conversation

*William H. Rickards, Jeana Abromeit, Marcia Mentkowski,
Heather Mernitz*

Abstract

*Higher education evaluation or assessment plans generally look to key assess-
ments within the curriculum for critical demonstrations of students' learning.
Increasingly, accreditation agencies (e.g., Southern Association of Schools and
Colleges, National Council on Accreditation of Teacher Education) have asked
for evidence of how faculty have made use of student outcome data in their own
ongoing planning. This is a condition that expands the notion of evaluation as a
collection of data from which to examine the merit or worth of a program to the
collaborative and analytic meaning making of evaluative action. This has been
an area of traditional complication where evaluators work to support the use of
evaluation findings while maintaining appropriate independence from the program administrators with operational responsibility. However, this combination
of instructional needs, accountability expectations, and insight into evaluative
outcomes amplifies the need for evaluator expertise for collaborating in these
dimensions of practice. This study then examines the work of a faculty and
its assessment team—including evaluation researchers—to (a) implement and
evaluate a general education program through a midprogram assessment, (b)
analyze the faculty's engagement with the results and (c) adapt the reporting and
meaning-making processes to further invest the faculty as coinvestigators in the
evaluation and its use in improving the program.* © 2016 Wiley Periodicals,
Inc., and the American Evaluation Association.

NEW DIRECTIONS FOR EVALUATION, no. 151, Fall 2016 © 2016 Wiley Periodicals, Inc., A Wiley Company, and
the American Evaluation Association.   Published online in Wiley Online Library (wileyonlinelibrary.com) • DOI:
10.1002/ev.20198

To Begin

After 15 years as a faculty member, the professor began to serve in senior administrative positions, eventually heading an office of faculty advancement. Looking back over decades of collaborative work, she reflected that she had seen the faculty participate in wonderful conversations about student learning and teaching practice. "These were conversations that moved our practice forward immensely," she said. "But you know, they were seldom anchored in data that we had analyzed on student performance. Really, it seems like the best conversations have not really involved empirical data on student performance, except through faculty expertise. In fact, the ones where we have reported summary scores on learning outcomes have sometimes seemed the least energetic … except for the ones where they were making links to key issues in practice."

In higher education, evaluation or assessment plans will generally look to key assessments within the curriculum for critical demonstrations of students' learning. From an evaluation perspective, there are at least three analytic questions that shape practice in the current context: How well did students perform? How trustworthy is the instrument or procedure? And how are the findings taken up by faculty?

Although the first two questions have been frequent topics of higher education scholarship, accreditation efforts have increasingly attended to how programs and institutions implement faculty processes for examining and making use of student outcome data. There is a persistent position that educational programs should be doing this and that educators have the appetite and skills to use such data. Yet in 3 decades of higher education assessment, there seems to be more about admonishing educators with select examples of good practice than critically examining the challenges confronted (e.g., compliance with the demands of external accountability vs. the need for internal curriculum study), whereas questions persist about how faculty will actually use such data (Banta & Pike, 2011; Peck, Gallucci, & Sloan, 2010).

This chapter examines the implementation of a key assessment at the middle of an undergraduate program to evaluate general student progress in quantitative and scientific literacy, including student ability with basic statistical skills and formulating research questions/hypotheses. Using data from two semesters of administration, the college's assessment council and office of educational research and evaluation collaborated on basic analysis and structured conversations with the college faculty to develop their deliberations on the outcomes. Then the chapter takes up the question of the assessment design team's metaevaluation of practice and the continuing revisions in both the instrument and the evaluation. What resulted from this review was an elaboration of an interactive evaluation model that led to a further conceptualization of the practice—one that explicates the evaluation role in relation to ongoing faculty development, collaborative

NEW DIRECTIONS FOR EVALUATION • DOI: 10.1002/ev

inquiry, and a more textured picture of the expertise of implementing the evaluation. After all, if faculty are to use evaluation results, what role does the evaluator have in anticipating and supporting such use? And how are evaluators prepared for such responsibilities?

Finally, the evaluation is described as an interactive process that built on multiple discussions and interpretations and ultimately touches on the three different but intertwined perspectives of student performance, instrument performance, and faculty deliberations on meaning and practice.

Context and Perspective

Frequently, assessment can function as a blunt instrument—assessment specialists gather data and present it to faculty with the presumption that it will be meaningful. In some cases, these involve broad outcomes like persistence, graduation rate, or postgraduate employment, which can speak to overall program effects but may have less significance, frankly, for instruction and curriculum. Even reported performance on an exam or other assessment instrument aimed at significant learning outcomes can be difficult for individual faculty members or departments to interpret if they are not involved in the specific course. General education coursework can be particularly difficult because faculty overall may feel less involved in broad outcomes than their specific course assignments. Nonetheless, those of us who have worked in varied capacities with communities of educators know how important the discourse can be when it touches on relations between effective practice and student learning.

The ability to use evaluation inquiry to enhance educational practice involves a clear understanding of how discursive aspects operate within a community of educators. From a similar perspective, utilization-focused evaluation has emphasized the importance of engaging program staff and practitioners who will make use of evaluative evidence and adequately linking evaluation processes with the actual work of the program (Patton, 2008). More problematically, faculty can find themselves as the object of an exercise in which they are asked to "close the loop" but without meaningful consequences or build a "culture of evidence" without adequate connections to available data (cf., Peck & McDonald, 2014).

In general, in higher education evaluations, faculty involvement is sought from the beginning, and there is attention to anticipated uses— that is, building on a perspective that knowledge of student performance will be of critical interest to educators and should provide actionable evidence for further developing practice. What may be problematic is the way in which group statistics and measures present abstractions in relation to the intentions and instructional practices in particular courses. The synthesis of data seems to operate at some distance from the teaching discourse of faculty, where evaluation and sense-making proceed. This lack of relevance seems to lead to judgmental claims about problems of practice where there is not enough context with the data to engage faculty from their individual, working positions (Banta & Pike, 2011). (See also Julnes, 2012, for additional perspectives on the problems of building evaluative reasoning in communities of practice.)

If the intent is to use student outcomes to contribute to the faculty's processes for monitoring and improving instructional quality, it is critical to examine specific elements and procedures:

- How does a community of educators review and monitor educational quality?
- How does it collect information about student work?
- How do the members examine and compare their own practices in order to think about which ones have the best impact or how, in fact, to improve upon practice? And what is known about their practical reasoning that leads to effective instructional practice?
- What kinds of data have been characteristic of their best discussions—for example, means scores, distributions, trends, abstract scores, or case examples contextualized by family practice?

The picture of faculty discourse that emerges from this perspective on practice suggests a need for something more complex than reporting results and emphasizes how evaluation logic is inherent and operates in the specific faculty's discourse on their practices. It suggests a progression of concerns for those who conduct evaluations and work to introduce their evidence into faculty practice:

- Refining the questions so that data can address meaningful concerns of faculty
- Understanding the practical discourse of teaching in order to present data and engage faculty in making meaning from data
- Sustaining evaluation and action research in order to move teaching learning practices forward

Data-Based Discussions and Higher Education Curriculum Development

Extensive scholarship in higher education learning, teaching, and curriculum has demonstrated the importance of using student performance data to examine learning theories at an institutional level (e.g., Kuh et al., 2015; Mentkowski & Associates, 2000). These have included the implementation of faculty frameworks for teaching and learning (McAlpine, Weston, Berthiaume, Fairbank-Roch, & Owen, 2004; Mentkowski & Associates, 2000; Saroyan, Weston, McAlpine, & Cowan, 2004) and how disciplines can operate as unique frameworks for learning and instructional practice (Riordan & Roth, 2004). Additionally, empirical studies of student outcomes and close analysis of faculty and institutional practice have provided great insight into teaching performance (Bain, 2004) and, more broadly, the powerful effects of curriculum principles and structures (Kuh, Kinzie, Schuh, Whitt, & Associates, 2005).

Three recent examples provide perspective on how the approach to structuring faculty review of student and program data become the basis for significant development.

Peck et al. (2010) have studied that how teacher education faculty make use of high-stakes performance assessment results in ongoing program development. They have been specifically concerned with how these discussions can be shifted from compliance-oriented activities—vis-a-vis accountability and accreditation standards—to inquiry activities where educators use the assessment data to investigate their own priority questions.

- Their studies reveal how the simple requirements of "use" can engender disconnection and a lack of investment, emphasizing compliance over the scholarship of educational work.
- They describe the importance of eliciting local questions, using inquiry to stimulate engagement between the data and the program; these are questions rooted in the needs of the program not the presumptions of the instruments.
- Alternatively, there is little attention yet to how faculty groups can vary in their actual approach to the data, how their reactions helped or hindered, and what steps were used to bridge the questions about practices (e.g., success in clinical supervision) and the data stored in high-stake assessments (e.g., candidate teacher portfolios and student test scores.) They present a powerful case for the role of evaluative inquiry but clearer understanding of the challenges and strategies of this approach is needed.

Bensimon and her colleagues (Bensimon, 2004; Bensimon & Chase, 2012; Bensimon & Dowd, 2012) have demonstrated how descriptive data on minority student representation—in figures such as admission statistics and completion rates—become a starting point for intense discussions on social equity when they are examined by faculty and administrators in the context of curriculum, practice, and policies. Their work has led to a range of strategies addressing organizational learning that support

- the use of an inquiry model to directly involve educators in meaning making related to available data (e.g., enrollment statistics, course syllabi, and program documents) and policy concerns; and
- the use of a workshop format to begin significant processes that can be sustained in various frameworks, to increase feasible implementation, and through the inquiry to forge a shared program of development.

Kezar's (2014) studies of how colleges change also speak to the critical operation of engagement and leadership in shaping institutional practice:

- Studying change involves understanding the forces and norms at play in the interacting cultures of higher education, but she has been particularly concerned with how the theoretical and conceptual understanding of higher education change provides frameworks for the multiple educator roles that are involved in leading change.
- Evaluation—as a practice of evaluators commissioned by faculty and administrators and as a practice pursued by educators in their varied spheres—is intensely conditioned by the perspectives that emerge from this complex understanding of higher education. The extent that evaluative activities will have impact on the quality of higher education is therefore related to the ability of evaluators and those who are using evaluation tactically and strategically.
- She has drawn attention to how sense-making—that is, the combined processes by which diverse participants collaborate in building the institutional community and culture—operates across the opportunities of academic life (e.g., from committees to curriculum planning to publishing). These are processes that can include extended discourse, shared research, coauthoring policy, and other interdepartmental faculty development.
- Specifically, she notes how the educational leaders who function as agents of changes need to recognize the complicated and layered nature of the contexts in which they are operating on campus and beyond. By extension, evaluators are operating under similar conditions and need a similar understanding of the contexts of higher education practice in which their work will have meaning.

Taken together, these perspectives emphasize how the work of evaluating a general education assessment can be constructed to advance the faculty's own examination of its principles and practices and how the evaluation researchers carry complex responsibilities into these inquiries.

Program Context

A Midwest college introduced an undergraduate midprogram assessment for all students, under the guidance of an assessment design team. The process was designed to address quantitative and scientific literacy outcomes from early coursework, including basic statistical skills and formulating research questions/hypotheses. The students came to the assessment having successfully completed three to five semesters; the assessment itself was a half-day event in which students reviewed materials and completed a written exam in which they developed a research approach to a specified problem; faculty from all departments assessed the students' performances. In

NEW DIRECTIONS FOR EVALUATION • DOI: 10.1002/ev

its final form, as developed by the design committee, the assessment consisted of a case presentation on water quality and consumer issues regarding bottled water, with relevant data on water contaminants. Students were required to calculate selected statistical analyses, interpret graphs, and develop appropriate research questions and hypotheses in relation to a given case. Student responses, assessor judgments and feedback, and students' self-assessments were collected electronically. What becomes noteworthy in this example is how the sustained collaboration of the faculty deepened the local understanding of how to use assessment activities to in program evaluation and shed light on the more general practices of engaging faculty—or other practitioners—in an evaluative conversation.

Data from two semesters of implementation—involving over 200 students—were analyzed to examine differences by demographics, major and faculty background, and presented in an all-college workshop. A significant majority of students demonstrated the targeted levels of performance; but the results also varied in meaningful ways among programs and provided a foundation for continuing questions regarding how various aspects of science and reasoning might be taught across varied programs. Faculty reviewed their data and talked with their department colleagues about the outcomes. They recorded their department-level observations and continuing questions to support subsequent analyses and deliberations. The assessment team provided descriptive statistics for various outcomes, but the intent was to help faculty connect the student performances with their curriculum intentions and instructional practices. Through this work, the evaluation practices could deepen and extend the educational innovations.

The school continued to use the assessment and provided data back to the departments. Within the assessment council, the design team for this assessment met periodically to review the results and oversee modification in the instrument and provided reports to the council and the faculty. Over time, the sustained reflections of faculty constituted a critique of the both the assessment and its processes of reporting and working with the results. From this perspective, it can be useful to think of the assessment council's work in three phases: one focused on descriptive reporting on student performance, a second concerned with critique and reflection to better understand faculty engagement, and a third designed to refine approaches to reporting and engaging faculty.

Approach and Method

In the initial phase, the council's interest was in understanding the student performance and synthesizing the data for the faculty. The primary analysis was a frequency count for item-level achievements. Additionally, individual item scores were then correlated with overall success on the assessment; the correlations were used in an exploratory analysis to consider difference among items and their place in the curriculum. After two

NEW DIRECTIONS FOR EVALUATION • DOI: 10.1002/ev

semesters of implementation, results were reviewed by the design team and considered from the general curriculum and departmental perspectives represented there. The team worked on how to make the most cogent presentation of data to the faculty at an all-college meeting that included time for department-level discussions. There, they examined their students' progress and reflected back on their courses that contributed to student learning in quantitative literacy and scientific reasoning.

Alongside this work, the assessment team was interested in documenting the implementation of the instrument, the program implementation, analyzing the reactions of faculty and students, and improving both the instrument and the evaluation practices that would enable learning for the faculty. In the second phase—critique and reflection—the analysis shifted to the experience of the faculty and how they made sense of student performance data. Data from faculty were collected directly through worksheets used in the faculty workshop in which departments met to review the student performances and potential implications. Subsequently, the council summarized the work in individual departments, continued discussions, and curriculum development.

In this regard, part of the data collection involved monitoring the faculty discussions themselves, at the department level as well as the assessment council and planning group. The minutes from these meetings as well as the observations constitute a record of how the process of meaning making emerged and how various approaches seemed to contribute to the discussions. Collected work over the next 2 years resulted in a clearer thinking about process that would allow faculty members to effectively engage student results and move into further analyses of curriculum and educational practice.

In the third phase, the observations from different sources were integrated into a workshop format that would link inquiry activities back to the classes and curriculum for continued use at the department level.

Results

In line with the overall project's intentions, the results are presented in terms of the student outcomes and the college's reflection on its own processes.

Descriptive Reporting

Overall, 78% of the students successfully completed the assessment on their first attempt. Although there was some variation among departments, these were not powerful enough to signal specific problems; they became a basis for faculty reflection on curriculum and courses. As a follow-up, the design team developed a workshop for students targeted to the learning outcomes that they would complete before taking a second assessment using a similar framework but different instrument and problem. Over 90% of the students were successful in the second assessment.

In terms of the instrument itself, the items were designed by mapping performance elements onto the quantitative elements (e.g., statistics, graph use, and scientific method) taught in various introductory courses required of all students. Faculty assessors were all required to participate in a training program that targeted the items and judgments of the instrument, with performance examples. A second assessor judged all students who were unsuccessful in the initial administration. A stratified sample of successful/not successful students was selected for review by two other reviewers, with an overall agreement of 85% on success.

The data from the initial assessments were analyzed, with basic descriptive statistics for overall success and item-level judgments and presented to faculty, with worksheets to help them in the meaning making. Specifically, they were asked to (a) look for patterns in their majors, for areas of particular strength and struggle; (b) identify relevant next steps for the department; and (c) note additional areas that the faculty might want to "address/raise/vent." They generally observed that the pass levels were consistent with their expectations although they could note areas that seemed to need specific attention in their introductory courses. They raised careful questions about how topic areas developed in their specific subjects could be addressed in courses. There were also some sharp reactions regarding validity and relevance in relation to their students and learning outcomes.

As the faculty continue their deliberations, the combined analysis of frequencies and correlations may become helpful, to the extent that such a comparison narrows attention to items that are both infrequently met and of particular significance to overall success. (See Table 4.1.)

In effect, the most frequently achieved items were of least consequence to the student's overall success; those with highest correlations showed lesser frequency of achievement, potentially pointing to classes or areas of the curriculum where intervention may be of more consequence. As noted in Table 4.2, the items that assessors most frequently judged as highly satisfactory were seldom those that correlated in a meaningful way with overall success (for example, correctly identifying factors from their calculations). Those that were least achieved offer some insights into what might be the target of curriculum change; however, those that have the strongest correlations with overall success may provide perhaps the strongest empirical base for curriculum discussions and revisions (for example, identifying alternative hypotheses).

Although the faculty are in a position to think about the results from their individual courses and learning activities, the assessment team in its evaluation is also in a position to use analysis to identify findings in relation to significant curriculum perspectives and to provide faculty—and departments—with the opportunities to take up these questions. In this case, for example, the observations regarding research questions—and how

Table 4.1. Distribution of Assessment Instrument Items by Frequency and Correlation with Overall Success

Correlation of Criteria Success with Overall Progress Code	Frequency of Assessor Judgments (Percentage Satisfactory for Criteria and Outcomes)		
	High 77%–94%	Moderate 60%–76%	Low 37%–59%
High ($r = 0.4$–0.8)	Frequently demonstrated and highly associated with overall success	Moderately demonstrated and highly associated with overall success	Infrequently demonstrated but highly associated with overall success
Moderate ($r = 0.2$–0.4)	Frequently demonstrated and moderately associated with overall success	Moderately demonstrated and moderately associated with overall success	Infrequently demonstrated and moderately associated with overall success
Low ($r < 0.2$)	Frequently demonstrated with little association with overall success	Moderately demonstrated with little association with overall success	Infrequently demonstrated with little association with overall success

Table 4.2. Comparing Correlations and Frequencies for Items in the Midprogram Assessment

Correlation of Criteria Success with Overall Progress Code	Frequency of Assessor Judgments (Percentage Satisfactory for Criteria and Outcomes)		
	High 77%–94%	Moderate 60%–76%	Low 37%–59%
High ($r = 0.4$–0.8)		Quality of self-assessment Explaining research question and testable hypotheses	Analyses of alternative hypotheses and implications
Moderate ($r = 0.2$–0.4)			Framing hypotheses, supportive analyses, and graph preparation
Low ($r < 0.2$)	Providing responses found in or directly calculated from the resource materials		Explaining data-based comparisons

students might be prepared for these and their foundations in quantitative representations—also touches on students learning about how ideas and conceptual frameworks interact. Dealing with research questions represents one application of this, but it operates in some form across all disciplines.

The design team continued its deliberations to address the best use of their evaluative practice. They were particularly concerned about the difficulties of some faculty in responding to performance data, the tentativeness of meaning making, and the challenges of collaborative evaluation inquiry within the available resources. Overall, these observations revealed concerns about how the evaluation practice needed to nurture an infrastructure for curriculum inquiry. They identified three topical areas that would become the basis for further evaluations:

- Articulated reporting in relation to faculty questions
- Meaning making that helped faculty make links between learner performance and instructional practice
- Engaging faculty as coinvestigators

Specifically, they were working to make student learning an empirical inquiry and make it possible to critically examine curriculum and instructional practices at a meaningful level.

Critique and Reflection

In the second phase, the worksheet responses as well as the observations at the departments and the council reflections pointed to distinct aspects of how faculty experienced the topics.

- Assessment statistics seem distant from meaningful practice for faculty members.
- Relationships to specific coursework or teaching practice were unclear.
- Questions about the assessment instrument and its trustworthiness ("What kind of meaning are we supposed to make of data from an instrument that doesn't have established validity?").
- There were feelings of puzzlement, not knowing what to do with much of the data, particularly if one is not involved in classes of specific relevance.

Alternatively, faculty show concern for and interest in

- how to help one another across departments.
- how to explore topics in their courses that will function in related areas. For example, developing skills in a math class for constructing and interpreting graphs supports their use in communicating concepts with different audiences in social sciences; identifying needs for quantitative

reasoning at a general education introductory level could strengthened its application prerequisite courses for a major.
- working between the interpretation of summary data on performances and the individual examples of performance that faculty work with in their classes.
- the importance of seeing performances in the context of the protocols used to elicit performances, the preparation students have had, and the judgments used by faculty assessors.

From the council's perspective, one of the persistent issues has been how to make data reporting a means to the conversations that faculty are ready to have—and need to have—regarding courses, curriculum, teaching, and learning. This is particularly so with tools and processes that can broadly be considered to be contextually relevant and trustworthy but don't have measurement properties. Additionally, the evolving nature of discussions and the efforts to adapt the assessment processes further make it difficult to closely monitor effects through statistical analysis, because changes in items, teaching practice, and curriculum are generally not systematic.

In sum, these findings help us address the questions of how we can evaluate student progress in specific areas through across multiple courses in the first years of the undergraduate program and how we can approach potential targets for further development in specific courses and programs. But the observations also point to how much the analysis and reporting can be a passive experience for faculty, even when there is considerable effort to support department level inquiry. But the implication here is that there is some shift in evaluator roles from presenting results to faculty as stakeholders—who receive and then use information—to investing faculty as agents who construct meaning from the data and build use into their interpretations. In this scenario, the evaluators and assessment team are rethinking how the data reporting is structured to maximize the direct involvement of faculty.

Engaging the Evaluative Conversation: Rethinking Evaluation Reporting

The importance of attending to evaluation reporting has been a persistent topic in evaluation practice, particularly from those who are concerned with the use of evaluation findings (e.g., King & Stevahn, 2013; Patton, 2008; Torres, Preskill, & Piontek, 2005). In higher education settings—perhaps because of the culture and the nature of the academic and pedagogical structures and the need for demonstrable improvement—it is possible to elaborate the potential models in relation to the evaluator roles and relations with faculty. Looking back over the reporting efforts regarding the mid-program assessment—as well as related efforts that informed our choices,

Table 4.3. Different Approaches to Evaluation Reporting and Evaluator Roles

Descriptive Reporting	Key Question Analysis	Engaging the Evaluation Conversation: Vesting Faculty as Coinquirers
Basic analysis of data from assessed performances	Tailored analysis for specific and anticipated question Support for interpretive and planning discussions with faculty	Using available program documents (e.g., syllabi and assessment plans) link assessed performances (data) and faculty discourse (meaning making) with course-based activities (praxis). Collaborate with faculty to identify further action research to support program quality.

the approaches to reporting fall into some broad categories as described in Table 4.3.

The first two of these involve faculty in relatively passive roles; the data are explained and reported, and so forth. In the second, broad knowledge of educational concerns is used to support further analysis of data by the assessment unit and will be accompanied by select questions. Faculty interpretations and applications and implications are sought as part of the consultation, but, as noted above, the efforts often do not result in significant engagement (cf., Banta & Pike, 2011; Peck et al., 2010). What is proposed, then, is a third alternative in which the overall act in which faculty actively become coinvestigators. This is a shift from their receiving analysis—in compliance with an institutional commitment to use data—to their becoming coconstructors of the analysis and interpretation. Additionally, such work needs to be pursued within the scarce time and human resources of department structures.

Experience in the midprogram assessment suggests that an effective step can begin with the available program documents and draw on the curriculum and instructional processes in individual departments, with the data presented in a workshop, faculty meeting, or similar context—that is, the syllabi for each of the department's courses that feed into the midprogram point. As faculty had the student performance data for review, they would participate in a mediated discussion that asked them to examine the linkages between the present data, the course-based activities with greatest relevance to these data, and their practical discourse on course planning and curriculum development. They can be asked to use the syllabi as a data set that can be investigated. With a template of questions, the faculty can explore the interplay among student data, meaning making, and praxis within their department structures with concrete opportunities for continued action research. These kinds of meetings can be held in the context of faculty meetings or development workshops, with potential opportunities for continuing action research.

Across various contexts, these meetings have included activities in which faculty collect data from their own practices in combination with student performance data and examine meaning and implications, shifting their roles from passive interpreters to coinvestigators. For example:

- Examining the links among the learning outcomes under study, the learning theories employed in the departments and courses, and the existing courses with potential relations
- Using program documents (e.g., course syllabi and assessment plans) to identify learning activities that might address the outcomes under study and related student work completed in class that might give insight to student readiness for the documented assessment
- In collaboration with the assessment or evaluation team, articulating the conversations that faculty use in the department to review course success and consider student performance
- Combining this knowledge with the current outcomes from student assessment, what questions could be studied in an action research format to move the department forward?

Additionally, in terms of reporting, these groups have produced a continuum of products from data-focused technical reports prepared by evaluators to published program research coauthored by evaluators and faculty.

Concluding Observations

In the context of this particular campus, the formalized review of assessment results implements the institution's commitment to its prime student learning commitments. However, a particular point to stress here is the extent to which evaluator expertise emerges beyond student design and data analysis in support of faculty deliberations—how reports are presented, the processes by which faculty engage the results, the extent that they are directly participating in interpreting and making use of instruments and evaluative data. As evaluators recognize and build on the interrelated concerns—of student performance, of instrument performance, curriculum-based evaluation—they increase the potential for supporting educational development.

This also means developing techniques for reporting that embed feasible inquiry activities in the opportunities for faculty interaction (e.g., reporting and development workshops that involve syllabus study and examination of teaching and learning cases). Additionally, it emphasizes the important role of evaluators in learning to work within the discourse practices of professional communities and adapt evaluation activities to support the work of those they are serving and their preparation for such roles. This is a shift in thinking about evaluation from analysis and design roles to more educator roles, facilitating the faculty members' use of evaluation logic and deeper study of student learning and instructional practice.

This necessarily includes professional development activities that facilitate faculty involvement as coinvestigators (e.g., articulating evaluation questions, interpreting data through curriculum and instruction, etc.). The examples here specifically deal with understanding how faculty—as the recipients of the evaluation evidence—deliberate on their practice and the key topics that organize their involvement with faculty, in areas such as student learning and performance, instructional practices, and an understanding of how the practical discourse of faculty serves as the context in which evaluation data contributes to developing practice. To the extent that these are significant elements in evaluations in higher education and related contexts, we also need to ask about the preparation or expertise of evaluators in these roles.

How do they understand the development of expertise in communities of practice?

How can they collaborate with faculty—and other practitioners—to design learning activities to facilitate analysis and interpretation of evaluation evidence in professional contexts?

How do they monitor and construct their own performance—as a metaevaluation—to balance the integrity and power of evaluation practice with the demands of the educational context?

References

Bain, K. (2004). *What the best college teachers do.* Cambridge, MA: Harvard University Press.

Banta, T., & Pike, G. (2011). The bottom line: Will faculty use assessment findings? In C. Secolsky & D. Denison (Eds.), *Handbook of measurement, evaluation and assessment in higher education* (pp. 47–56). New York, NY: Routledge.

Bensimon, E. M. (2004). The Diversity Scorecard: A learning approach to institutional change. *Change: The Magazine of Higher Learning. 36*(1), 44–52.

Bensimon, E. M., & Chase, M. M. (2012). Equity Scorecard for higher education. In J. A. Banks (Ed.), *Encyclopedia of diversity in education* (pp. 813–817). Thousand Oaks, CA: Sage.

Bensimon, E. M., & Dowd, A. C. (2012). *Developing the capacity of faculty to become institutional agents for Latinos in STEM.* Los Angeles, CA: University of Southern California.

Julnes, G. (Ed.). (2012). *New Directions for Evaluation: No. 133. Promoting valuation in the public interest: Informing policies for judging value in evaluation.* San Francisco: Jossey-Bass.

Kezar, A. (2014). *How Colleges Change.* New York, NY: Routledge.

King, J. A., & Stevahn, L. (2013). *Interactive evaluation practice: Mastering the interpersonal dynamics of program evaluation.* Newbury Park, CA: Sage.

Kuh, G. D., Ikenberry, S. O., Jankowski, N. A., Cain, T. R., Ewell, P. T., Hutchings, P., & Kinzie, J. (2015). *Using evidence of student learning to improve higher education.* New York, NY: Wiley.

Kuh, G. D., Kinzie, J., Schuh, J. H., Whitt, E. J., & Associates (2005). *Student success in college: Creating conditions that matter.* San Francisco, CA: Jossey-Bass.

McAlpine, L., Weston, C., Berthiaume, D., Fairbank-Roch, G., & Owen, M. (2004). Reflection on teaching: Types and goals of reflection. *Educational Research and Evaluation. 10*(4–6), 337–363.

Mentkowski, M., & Associates. (2000). *Learning that lasts: Integrating learning, development, and performance in college and beyond.* San Francisco, CA: Jossey-Bass.

Patton, M. Q. (2008). *Utilization-focused evaluation* (4th ed.). Thousand Oaks, CA: Sage.

Peck, C. A., Gallucci, C., & Sloan, T. (2010). Negotiating implementation of high stakes performance assessment policies in teacher education: From compliance to inquiry. *Journal of Teacher Education. 61*(5), 451–463.

Peck, C. A., & McDonald, M. (2014). What is a culture of evidence? How do you get one? And…should you want one? *Teachers College Record. 116*(3). Retrieved from http://www.tcrecord.org. ID Number: 17359.

Riordan, T., & Roth, R. (Eds.). (2004). *Disciplines as frameworks for student learning: Teaching the practice of the disciplines.* Herndon, VA: Stylus.

Saroyan, A., Weston, C., McAlpine, L., & Cowan, S. (2004). The final step: Evaluation of teaching. In A. Saroyan & C. Amundsen (Eds.), *Rethinking teaching in higher education: From a course design workshop to a faculty development framework* (pp. 115–130). Sterling, VA: Stylus.

Torres, R., Preskill, H., & Piontek, M. E. (2005). *Evaluation strategies for communicating and reporting: Enhancing learning in organizations* (2nd ed.). Thousand Oaks, CA: Sage.

WILLIAM H. RICKARDS *is a consultant at Independent Evaluation Inquiry.*

JEANA ABROMEIT *is a professor of sociology at Alverno College.*

MARCIA MENTKOWSKI *is professor emerita of psychology at Alverno College.*

HEATHER MERNITZ *is an associate professor of physical science at Alverno College.*

NEW DIRECTIONS FOR EVALUATION • DOI: 10.1002/ev

Stitt-Bergh, M. (2016). Assessment capacity building at a research university. In W. H. Rickards, & M. Stitt-Bergh (Eds.), *Evaluating student learning in higher education: Beyond the public rhetoric. New Directions for Evaluation, 151,* 69–83.

Assessment Capacity Building at a Research University

Monica Stitt-Bergh

Abstract

Higher education institutions use program-level learning outcomes assessment to improve programs, enhance student learning, and meet external requirements. An assessment office at a research university used a variety of evaluation capacity-building (ECB) activities to increase faculty and administrators' engagement in assessment and use of findings for program improvement. To investigate six desired ECB outcomes, the author analyzed survey responses and program assessment reports (2008–2014). The findings showed success in four ECB outcomes: positive attitudes toward assessment, motivation to engage, knowledge and skills, and department climate. However, two outcomes fell below expectations: department resources and use of findings. A correlation study revealed several significant, positive relationships between outcomes and faculty engagement with the strongest relationship being between level of faculty assessment experience and knowledge and skills. Because use of findings for program improvement and better student learning are primary assessment purposes, these results are valuable for campus planning of future capacity-building activities. New ECB efforts that focus on faculty capacity to discuss assessment with colleagues, department resources, and most important, ways to use assessment findings are planned. © 2016 Wiley Periodicals, Inc., and the American Evaluation Association.

Evaluation capacity building (ECB) is an excellent choice for evaluators working with higher education institutions to help them improve programs and meet accountability requirements. Labin, Duffy, Meyers, Wandersman, and Lesesne (2012) define ECB as "an intentional process to increase individual motivation, knowledge, and skills, and to enhance a group or organization's ability to conduct or use evaluation" (p. 308). ECB's goal is to integrate evaluation practice into program operations and habits of mind so it becomes sustainable (Preskill & Boyle, 2008). ECB typically involves evaluation experts facilitating learning experiences such as training and mentoring as well as written materials and technology. It often takes a participatory approach through which an expert collaborates with program personnel on evaluation activities. By bringing personnel together to participate in evaluation activities and reflect on program implementation, ECB is designed to increase program and organizational learning. The ECB literature indicates that ECB can result in increased knowledge about evaluation, improved skills related to conducting evaluation, and positive beliefs about evaluation.

ECB is ideal in higher education. The ECB emphasis on helping an organization conduct evaluation and use the results aligns with higher education regional and professional accreditation requirements that mandate student learning outcomes assessment at the program and institutional level. Student learning outcomes assessment (LOA) is a form of outcome evaluation in which findings about student learning are used for program or institutional improvement, with the emphasis on improvement. All regional accreditors in the United States require that institutions and their undergraduate and graduate degree programs establish learning outcomes, engage in ongoing program and institutional LOA, and use findings for improvement. All but one regional accreditor explicitly states that faculty be involved in the process (Provezis, 2010). ECB, by design, addresses the characteristics of LOA that accreditation standards specify and the assessment literature describe: formative, utilization focused, and actively involving faculty.

ECB fits university culture, and a research university in particular, with its tenets of academic freedom, peer evaluation practices, and disciplinary differences. ECB builds faculty capacity, and when faculty plan and conduct LOA, they do so in ways that maintain their academic freedom. ECB capitalizes on faculty's strong belief that they are in the best position to evaluate student performance and program effectiveness. And ECB can be tailored to address disciplinary differences that exist across a university campus.

In a 2014 forum on ECB in the *American Journal of Evaluation*, a cross-cutting theme was the call for more research on ECB (Leviton, 2014; Preskill, 2014; Suarez-Balcazar & Taylor-Ritzler, 2014), and this chapter, in part, answers that call. The higher education setting allows researchers a fresh venue to examine how evaluators assist faculty in LOA and the conditions in which an ECB approach may flourish.

NEW DIRECTIONS FOR EVALUATION • DOI: 10.1002/ev

This chapter reports on one research university's ECB efforts to improve degree programs and simultaneously respond to external accountability requirements. Prior to the regional accreditor's LOA requirement, the faculty and the institution relied on individual student course grades and student surveys as the student learning indicators. When the faculty and institution needed to produce program and institutional indicators of learning because of a 2002 change in external requirements, a major shift began. Between 2002 and 2008, the institution used various techniques such as guest speakers and minigrants that had modest success. In 2008, ECB became a primary component in moving LOA forward across all academic programs. This study investigated whether 6 years of capacity-building efforts were successful in creating a positive attitude toward LOA, increasing individual faculty knowledge and skills, and increasing program-level assessment activities.

Method

This study took place at a research university accredited by the WASC Senior College and University Commission (WSCUC). The university has more than 200 degree programs, of which 56 have professional accreditation, and roughly 2,000 faculty and 20,000 students; it is classified as a doctoral university, highest research activity, and high undergraduate enrollment. I draw on the integrative ECB model by Labin et al. (2012) to examine ECB in a university setting. The integrative ECB model includes three main areas: need, activities, and results.

ECB Need—Why

This university's primary motivation for building faculty capacity is to support faculty in their efforts to use learning outcomes assessment (LOA) for program improvement, which in turn would help meet external accreditation requirements. The campus administration had LOA on the radar since 2002 and initially promoted LOA through occasional visiting speakers and internal grant initiatives. The constant pressure from both external accreditors and the campus administration led the faculty to demand more assistance and guidance: a faculty senate task force asked for and received an assessment support office in 2008.

The assessment office opened amid great fear of assessment by faculty, specifically concerns that the federal regulations for K–12 education in the United States (e.g., No Child Left Behind) would expand into higher education, resulting in loss of academic freedom and improper use of results. Although campus administrators supported assessment and provided resources, the departmental culture was grim regarding LOA. To address the challenges, the assessment office drew from ECB as well as participatory evaluation, utilization-focused evaluation, and social constructivist theories

New Directions for Evaluation • DOI: 10.1002/ev

of learning (e.g., begin with prior knowledge and address misconceptions) to develop an ECB program for administrators and faculty.

The ECB program objectives for campus administrators were necessarily different from those for faculty. Leadership needed basic knowledge about what "counted" as LOA, an awareness of necessary resources, how to structure LOA within a program, motivate faculty, and support the use of findings. In contrast, because faculty do the heavy lifting, they needed to know LOA in greater detail, from planning to use. The ECB efforts for faculty were designed to help them

- conduct program-level learning outcomes assessment;
- perceive assessment as useful and meaningful;
- gain technical expertise in developing measurable learning outcomes, choosing appropriate data collection and analysis methods, and using findings for program improvement; and
- locate assessment-related resources—including faculty colleagues and examples of good assessment practices on campus.

To initially craft and then continually evolve the capacity-building efforts, the assessment office used an annual needs assessment survey, an analysis of the previous year's annual assessment reports, and accreditation requirements.

ECB Activities—What and How

The assessment office created a multimodal ECB approach that included face-to-face sessions and online and printed materials on the how and why of LOA. ECB included formal training and hands-on experiential learning as the literature has stressed its importance (Akintobi et al., 2012; Arnold, 2006; Garcia-Iriarte, Suarez-Balcazar, Taylor-Ritzler, & Luna, 2011; Huffman, Thomas, & Lawrenz, 2008; King & Volkov, 2005; Satterlund, Treiber, Kipke, Kwon, & Cassady, 2013). Training also included opportunities for structured and unstructured faculty discussions and activities in which faculty made connections to their degree program or curriculum to encourage learning transfer. The knowledge and skill building included the ability to develop evaluation questions, create measurable outcomes, align program activities with outcomes, design an LOA project, collect and analyze data, and use results for program improvement.

The assessment office asked that one faculty member from each program be the lead assessment person who would learn and then champion and coordinate LOA activities. They were one of the groups the office targeted for ECB. Between 2008 and 2014, the assessment office held regular face-to-face sessions and events:

- 63 capacity-building workshops on general topics (75 minutes each)
- 31 capacity-building workshops on specific topics based on program needs and open to select groups of faculty (60–90 minutes each)
- Two assessment leadership institutes that were supplemented by small group sessions (a 3-day institute and three subsequent 60-minute sessions)
- Four poster sessions in which faculty were recruited to present and were assisted in creating their posters
- More than 200 technical assistance consultations (60 minutes each)
- Annual presentations to deans/directors and biannual workshops for new deans/directors in order to build administrator capacity (15–60 minutes each)
- Five workshops by visiting experts (one full-day, one half-day, and three 90-minute sessions)

Over 500 faculty (25% of all faculty) participated in at least one of these capacity-building events.

In conjunction with these ECB activities, the assessment office worked with campus administrators and faculty senate leaders. The campus developed policies on the roles and responsibilities for LOA and added LOA to the existing college review procedures. The faculty senate created a standing committee on assessment. Administration approved ongoing funding for the assessment office, which covers two full-time positions, incentives for faculty to attend the 3-day institute, and office expenditures. The office has technical support for an online report submission system and a website. Administrative leaders speak at annual campuswide LOA events and the annual 3-day assessment institute, and at least two times each year they update the directors and deans and encourage LOA. Since 2008, the administration has sent a consistent, positive message to the faculty about assessment.

Evaluation of ECB

Three main sources of evidence were used to evaluate ECB and study the impact of the ECB efforts. First, between 2008 and 2014, attendees at workshops, events, and consultations completed surveys: all surveys contained questions on perceived learning, usefulness, and satisfaction, and the workshop surveys also included quiz questions to test attendee knowledge. The workshops averaged 19 participants per session and the survey return rate was 85% (1,069 surveys submitted).

Second, in September 2014, the assessment office distributed an Assessment Office Survey (AOS) to 266 faculty who had served as the lead assessment coordinators for their program between 2008 and 2014. The return rate was 62%. The respondents represented 90% of the departments and 100% of the university's colleges/schools. Fifty-eight percent were from arts and sciences, and 42% were from professional programs. Twenty-six percent of the respondents were in a professionally accredited program (e.g., engineering, law, and medicine) that has additional LOA requirements and standards apart from the university's.

The AOS was based on the Evaluation Capacity Assessment Instrument (ECAI; Taylor-Ritzler, Suarez-Balcazar, Garcia-Iriarte, Henry, & Balcazar, 2013) and evaluation conceptual models (Bourgeois, 2008; Labin et al., 2012; Preskill & Boyle, 2008). Pilot testing the ECAI led to changes to fit the context of higher education and terminology (e.g., "assessment" replaced "evaluation," "department chair" replaced "manager," and "faculty" replaced "staff"). The AOS had 74 questions pertaining to six dimensions: (a) Thoughts About Student Learning Outcomes Assessment ($\alpha = 0.95$), (b) Motivation to Engage in Student Learning Outcomes Assessment ($\alpha = 0.94$), (c) Knowledge and Skills ($\alpha = 0.96$), (d) Climate for Student Learning Outcomes Assessment in Your Department ($\alpha = 0.96$), (e) Resources for Student Learning Outcomes Assessment in Your Department ($\alpha = 0.87$), and (f) Use of Student Learning Outcomes Assessment Findings ($\alpha = 0.94$). Depending on the dimension, the respondents selected from these response options: strongly disagree, somewhat disagree, somewhat agree, and strongly agree (dimensions 1, 2, 4, and 5); not at all, to some extent, to a considerable extent, and to a very great extent (dimensions 3 and 6). Dimension five included a "do not know" option. The AOS was not anonymous and the last section contained background questions.

The third source of evidence was the annual program LOA reports submitted by degree program assessment coordinators: these were compared across time (2008–2014) on factors such as completion, type of evidence collected, and use of findings for program improvement. The number of degree programs at the university ranged from 224 in 2008 to 238 programs in 2014.

Results

The evidence collected shed light on outcomes for individual faculty members and organizational and program outcomes. Correlation revealed the strength of relationships between variables such as the years of involvement with LOA and the department climate.

Individual-Level Outcomes

At the individual level, the ECB efforts were designed to increase knowledge and skill, foster a positive attitude toward LOA, and provide faculty assessment coordinators with tools to lead assessment projects in their program. The surveys given after a workshop, event, and consultation indicated that the ECB efforts were successful on individual outcomes. However, the AOS survey given in 2014 revealed several areas in need of improvement.

NEW DIRECTIONS FOR EVALUATION • DOI: 10.1002/ev

Table 5.1. Summary of Workshop and Consultation Survey Results

Workshop Outcome	Percentage of Respondents (N = 1069)
Useful	95% ("useful" and "very useful")
Effective in increasing understanding	89% ("effective" and "very effective")
Demonstrated knowledge (via quiz questions)	85% correctly answered

Consultation Outcome	Percentage of Respondents (N = 161)
Worthwhile	99%
Satisfaction with quality of information received	98% ("satisfied" and "very satisfied")

Figure 5.1. Mean score for each dimension on the Assessment Office Survey (AOS)

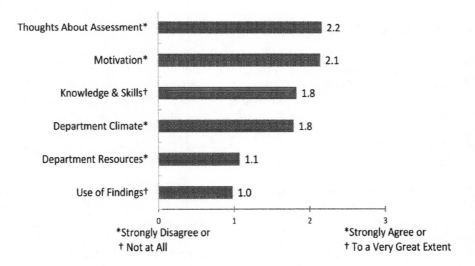

The workshop survey respondents overwhelming reported the session was useful and effective in increasing understanding of the workshop topic (Table 5.1). The workshop survey also included quiz questions to test knowledge and most attendees answered correctly. The technical assistance consultations were also viewed positively by the attendees in terms of the consultation being worthwhile and the quality of the information they received (Table 5.1).

The AOS distributed in the sixth year (2014) of the ECB efforts contained three dimensions related to individual outcomes: *Thoughts About Student Learning Outcomes Assessment, Motivation to Engage,* and *Knowledge and Skills.* The mean scores for the *Thoughts* and *Motivation* dimensions were the highest of all six dimensions on the AOS (Figure 5.1). The mean of score "2" corresponds to "somewhat agree." The mean scores for *Thoughts* ($M = 2.2$, $SD = 0.65$) and *Motivation* ($M = 2.1$, $SD = 0.85$) indicated the assessment coordinators were somewhat positive and motivated. The mean score for the *Knowledge and Skills* dimension ($M = 1.8$, $SD = 0.75$) falls just below "a considerable extent" (score $= 2$).

Within these dimensions, analysis of individual survey items provided more details. At least three quarters of the respondents somewhat agreed and strongly agreed with all of the items in the *Thoughts* and *Motivation* dimensions. On the other hand, none of the survey items in the *Knowledge and Skills* dimension had three quarters reporting considerable and extensive knowledge. The areas of most need pertained to developing and leading assessment projects: only half of the respondents indicated considerable and extensive knowledge and skill. On a positive note, two thirds reported considerable/extensive knowledge and skills in creating measurable learning outcomes and curriculum maps.

Organizational and Program Outcomes

Desired organizational outcomes of ECB include processes, policies, and practices; supportive leadership; a culture committed to learning and using data; mainstreaming evaluation; and evaluation resources (Labin et al., 2012). These are required for sustained evaluation practice (Preskill & Boyle, 2008). At the organizational level at this university, faculty government has approved two policies on assessment, the leadership concretely signaled LOA importance at assessment events, and the campus provided resources for a central assessment office and technology support.

The AOS included three dimensions related to program-level outcomes: *Climate for Student Learning Outcomes Assessment in Your Department*, *Resources for Student Learning Outcomes*, and *Use of Student Learning Outcomes Assessment Findings*. The mean scores (Figure 5.1) revealed that faculty respondents perceived *Department Climate* as lower than ideal given the mean score ($M = 1.8$) fell below "somewhat agree"; *Department Resources* were lacking ($M = 1.1$, "somewhat disagree"); and *Use of Findings* was low ($M = 1.0$), that is, findings used "to some extent" ($SDs = 0.7$).

The individual survey items in these dimensions pointed out particular strengths and weaknesses. The respondents perceived that their departments fostered a climate in which they were part of the decision making and encouraged to participate in assessment, but the environment was such that faculty did not know how assessment results would be used, and it was not easy to meet to discuss assessment. The perception was that department resources for assessment were limited: faculty were not compensated or provided time to participate in assessment. On a positive note, they perceived assessment expertise was available to them, along with technology. The results from the *Use of Findings* dimension suggested that assessment was not achieving its primary purpose to provide information for program improvement and better student learning. Only one third reported using findings to

Table 5.2. Outcomes and Curriculum Alignment in 2008 and 2014

	Percentage of Programs	
Program Activity	2008 (N = 224)	2014 (N = 238)
Established measurable learning outcomes	77%	98%
Published learning outcomes for stakeholders	60%	96%
Aligned curriculum and learning outcomes	41%	87%

Table 5.3. Evidence, Findings, and Use of Findings in 2011* and 2014

	Percentage of Programs	
Program Activity	2011 (N = 230)	2014 (N = 238)
Collected evidence	65%	75%
Reported findings	59%	66%
Described use of findings	51%	66%

*2011 is used as the comparison year because in 2011 reporting procedures changed and that prevented an accurate comparison to 2008.

make changes to the curriculum and only half reported using assessment to evaluate whether students met learning outcomes.

Another piece of evidence related to program outcomes is the annual LOA reports that programs submit to the assessment office. An analysis of these reports showed substantial growth in reported activities since ECB started in 2008 (Tables 5.2 and 5.3). The analysis also corroborated results from the AOS: program learning outcomes and curriculum alignment (through curriculum mapping) were higher whereas reporting and using findings were lower.

Relationships Between ECB and Outcomes

The AOS included survey items on the respondent's years of experience with LOA and participation in ECB activities, and these responses allowed an investigation of the relationships between the six dimensions and LOA engagement (Table 5.4). The strongest relationship by far was faculty's reported level of assessment experience and *Knowledge and Skills* ($R = 0.76$, $N = 164, p < .01$). Several significant, moderate, positive relationships also emerged: frequency of assessment discussions with colleagues and each of the six dimensions on the AOS ($Rs = 0.41$ to $.52, Ns = 159$ to $161, p < .01$); percentage of work related to assessment and *Department Climate, Department Resources*, and *Use of Findings* ($Rs = 0.44$ to $0.49, Ns = 161$ to 163, $p < .01$); noncampus ECB event attendance and *Knowledge and Skills* ($R = 0.51, N = 162, p < .01$); number of department meetings and *Department Climate* ($R = 0.48, N = 164, p < .01$). Other relationships were weak: years involved, on-campus ECB event attendance, LOA scholarly activities, and

Table 5.4. Correlation Matrix: Relationship of LOA Engagement and AOS Dimensions

Learning Outcomes Assessment (LOA) Experience/ Participation	Assessment Office Survey (AOS) Dimensions					
	Thoughts About LOA	Motivation to Engage	Knowledge and Skills	Dept. Climate	Dept. Resources	Use of Findings
Frequency of assessment discussions with colleagues	.43**	.44**	.41**	.52**	.41**	.44**
Percentage of work related to assessment	.33**	.30**	.35**	.45**	.44**	.49**
Number of department meetings on assessment-related issues	.29**	.23**	.16*	.48**	.34**	.40**
Level of experience with assessment	.24**	.15	.76**	.36**	.32**	.34**
Years involved with assessment in department	.04	.06	.39**	.25**	.13	.25**
Events/workshops attended: campus sponsored	.24**	.17*	.39**	.13	.17*	.10
Events/workshops attended: noncampus sponsored	.21**	.19*	.51**	.29**	.32**	.34**
Number of LOA scholarly activities	.29**	.29**	.36**	.15	.09	.22**
Number of times department completed assessment cycle	.08	.01	−.03	.16*	−.08	.12

**Correlation is significant at the 0.01 level (2-tailed).
*Correlation is significant at the 0.05 level (2-tailed).
$N = 161–164$.

the number of times the department completed the assessment cycle were not strongly related to the six dimensions.

Between dimensions, *Department Climate* and *Use of Findings* had a strong positive relationship ($R = 0.77$, $N = 162$, $p < .01$). *Department Climate* and *Department Resources* were also strongly related ($R = 0.66$, $N = 164$, $p < .01$) as were *Thoughts* and *Motivation* ($R = 0.74$, $N = 163$, $p < .01$).

NEW DIRECTIONS FOR EVALUATION • DOI: 10.1002/ev

Programs with professional accreditation (e.g., architecture, education, and medicine) have additional, externally mandated LOA requirements. The faculty in these programs had higher mean scores on the AOS than faculty in nonprofessionally accredited programs. The following were statistically significant (p < .01; Mann–Whitney U): *Department Resources* (professionally accredited group had a 0.6 higher mean score on a 4-point scale), *Use of Findings* (0.6 higher), *Knowledge and Skills* (0.5 higher), and *Department Climate* (0.4 higher). There were no significant differences in *Thoughts* and *Motivation* between faculty in and not in a professionally accredited program.

Discussion

After 6 years of intentional ECB activities at the university in this study, sustainable evaluation practices are visible. The university has institutionalized LOA through policies related to ownership and responsibility, administrator encouragement, standardized reporting procedures, a support office, and technology to streamline procedures and disseminate assessment information. The percentage of programs regularly carrying out assessment activities steadily increased. Most of the lead assessment coordinators share positive thoughts about assessment and are motivated to engage; most have some knowledge and skills but not in all areas of LOA. The results from the *Department Climate* dimension on the AOS indicate success in this area with room for improvement. This bodes well for the assessment office's plan for ongoing cultivation of key faculty who rotate the lead position so that LOA is eventually diffused throughout the programs (Garcia-Iriarte et al., 2011), and as lead faculty coordinators exit that role, others will be willing to take their place. A conducive assessment environment is needed for permeation to be successful.

Despite these indicators of success, this university falls short in department resources and use of findings, two extremely important areas. First, most respondents on the AOS reported that faculty do not have resources: insufficient time to participate and inadequate clerical support for LOA. The institutional investment in centralized resources and designation of lead faculty assessment coordinators are necessary but cannot carry the load. Second, 66% of programs reporting they used assessment findings for program decision making. This actually comes as little surprise given the frequent references to lack of use in the evaluation literature, as well as recurrent mentions about faculty resistance to LOA in the assessment literature (e.g., Section 1 introduction in Banta, 1999; Tagg, 2012) and the vocal opponents to LOA in articles titled *The Great Assessment Diversion* (Kelly-Woessner, 2011) and *Outcomes Assessment: No Gain, All Pain* (Fryshman, 2007). This study strongly suggests that the university concentrate ECB efforts on department resource strategies and how to use findings in its future ECB activities.

Effective ECB in Higher Education

This study's findings support the ECB model (Labin et al., 2012) and offer guidance for those developing ECB programs, particularly in higher education. Having time to do assessment was a primary resource need identified in this study, but the results also suggested that faculty do not want to spend more than 20% of their time on LOA activities. Faculty typically want to spend their time working with "clients" (the students) and on their own research rather than on program evaluation/assessment activities. An ECB program in higher education can benefit from addressing workload management and how to divide LOA responsibilities among program personnel. The organization should be aware of overtaxing these "accidental evaluators" (King & Volkov, 2005, p. 10) so the ones assigned lead responsibility do not suffer burnout or receive looks of pity from colleagues. Limiting an individual's work on assessment by distributing the workload has a trade-off: ECB facilitators will need to provide regular training aimed at beginners as well as those with advanced knowledge. Administrative solutions to the time issue include course release time, summer stipends, workload recognition, and credit for LOA in personnel evaluations (it is typically not included as part of faculty performance reviews).

An ECB program needs to adapt to meet new demands (Akintobi et al., 2012; Satterlund et al., 2013) and this was true at this university. Over time, ECB efforts changed to address more sophisticated evaluation topics as individual and organization learning occurred. Initial efforts laid the foundation—policies, philosophy, basic concepts—and later efforts addressed sustainability, reliability, standard setting, use of results. The multipronged ECB effort also included multiple formats of delivery (in person, online, phone, small group, large group, formal, informal), it targeted faculty and leadership, offered planned events, and held "just-in-time" or "real-time" consultations (Arnold, 2006).

An ECB program in higher education, particularly at research universities, can capitalize on certain aspects of the culture and context, which is what the focal university in this study did. First, the target group whose capacity is being increased is highly educated and often experienced in research, data analysis/interpretation, and the application of theory. They are resident experts (Cousins & Bourgeois, 2014). During ECB, facilitators can draw parallels between the faculty's existing skills and the skills needed in assessment in order to enable understanding, dispel misperceptions, and increase faculty confidence in their ability to implement assessment. Second, to encourage buy-in, ECB facilitators can reference the peer review model in higher education as an example of how faculty already participate in and support faculty-led evaluation of programs and institutions. In addition, faculty value their peers' expert advice. An ECB program that focuses on training respected faculty who then work with colleagues capitalizes on this faculty-to-faculty credibility. Third, at some campuses, faculty have a voice in program decisions and campus government that can promote assessment as a change agent because individuals are already empowered. However, faculty autonomy and ability to control their own work can lead to prioritizing personal goals rather than program outcomes. ECB facilitators can find themselves walking a fine line between faculty's academic freedom and program's collective objectives. Clearly, an understanding of academic freedom is crucial for evaluators. Finally, at other campuses, faculty have less control—perhaps no voice in decision making—and these faculty may be part of the ever-growing number of adjunct, nontenure track, and part-time faculty. This group, who likely teach many of a program's core courses and students, may be left out of assessment planning or asked to participate without compensation, neither of which bodes well for meaningful LOA or for use of findings to improve curriculum and instruction. ECB facilitators in this case face greater obstacles to faculty engagement (see Kezar & Maxey, 2014).

Current regional accreditation requirements and many professional accreditation requirements judge the campus on whether the LOA findings were used for program and institutional decision making: the use of findings may be more important than the findings themselves. Thus, LOA can be described as assessment for learning, not only assessment of learning. An effective ECB program can promote use and draw from the evaluation literature for guidance, for example, utilization-focused evaluation (Patton, 2008). It can address meaningful evaluation questions, appropriate data collection and analysis, and actionable findings and this is one step toward assisting with faculty and program staff with use. The assessment literature does not typically draw upon the evaluation field literature; doing so is strongly recommended, especially in the area of use.

One reason for the lack of use may be uncertainty about what action to take. Knowing that a particular outcome needs improvement is different from knowing what specific action will likely lead to actual improvement on that outcome. In general, evaluators may not be able to assist with the use of findings if they need particular content knowledge to develop an effective improvement plan. For example, in higher education, most faculty are not experts in learning theory and curriculum design. They may discover through LOA that students are weak on one learning outcome; however, they may not know which action will likely lead to increased outcome achievement. It is at this point that experts in cognitive and affective development and instructional design are needed, not experts in evaluation. Experts in learning theory may be the best option to help the evaluator and faculty craft a plan to improve learning outcomes when student achievement falls below standards. Thus, an ECB program in higher education may be most effective when it includes strategies for use that include knowing when to seek other expert help because an assessment project is considered finished only when the program uses the findings.

NEW DIRECTIONS FOR EVALUATION • DOI: 10.1002/ev

In regard to evaluating an ECB program, the existing conceptual models and instruments (Cousins & Bourgeois, 2014; Labin et al., 2012; Preskill & Boyle, 2008; Taylor-Ritzler et al., 2013) are useful. In general, ECB functions in the same manner across sectors and those who take an ECB approach face similar challenges and can use similar strategies to address them. The subtle differences caused by higher education culture and context, however, cannot be overlooked. An ECB program and those who run it need to be perceived as credible and trustworthy by the targeted groups for ECB to reach its goal of sustainable evaluation practice. Thus, the evaluator should engage in conversations with faculty in regards to credible findings and be willing to support the faculty's conception of appropriate evidence and so forth.

This study took place at a traditional research university with a unionized faculty. Other types of educational institutions and contexts face challenges such as faculty in different time zones and an increasing proportion of the part-time and nontenure-track instructors. Understanding the differences in thoughts, knowledge, participation, and motivation by faculty position type and tenure status is critical. All faculty and instructors need a safe space to conduct and discuss LOA. Kezar & Maxey (2014) describe the changes in higher education employment and provide recommendations to facilitate LOA when nontenure-track faculty are a large group on campus—important considerations if designing an ECB program for that context.

The higher education setting is an interesting and appropriate context to investigate and implement ECB. External accountability pressure paired with financial constraints have made ECB necessary in higher education. ECB has the potential to thrive because the faculty (the "program staff") have research expertise and the culture in higher education values peer review and faculty control of the curriculum—which the assessment results will inform.

References

Akintobi, T. H., Yancey, E. M., Daniels, P., Mayberry, R. M., Jacobs, D., & Berry, J. (2012). Using evaluability assessment and evaluation capacity-building to strengthen community-based prevention initiatives. *Journal of Health Care for the Poor and Underserved*. 23(2), 33–48.

Arnold, M. E. (2006). Developing evaluation capacity in extension 4-H field faculty: A framework for success. *American Journal of Evaluation*. 27(2), 257–269.

Banta, T. W. (1999). *Assessment update: The first ten years*. San Francisco, CA: Jossey-Bass.

Bourgeois, I. (2008). *Understanding the dimensions of organizational evaluation capacity* (Doctoral dissertation). Retrieved from ProQuest Dissertations & Theses Global. (Order No. NR48389).

Cousins, J. B., & Bourgeois, I. (2014). Cross-case analysis and implications for research, theory, and practice. In J. B. Cousins & I. Bourgeois, *New Directions for Evaluation: No. 141. Organizational capacity to do and use evaluation* (pp. 101–119). San Francisco, CA: Jossey-Bass.

Fryshman, B. (2007, November 13). Outcomes assessment: No gain, all pain. *Inside Higher Education*. Retrieved from https://www.insidehighered.com/views/2007/11/13/fryshman

Garcia-Iriarte, E., Suarez-Balcazar, Y., Taylor-Ritzler, T., & Luna, M. (2011). A catalyst-for-change approach to evaluation capacity building. *American Journal of Evaluation. 32*(2), 168–182.

Huffman, D., Thomas, K., & Lawrenz, F. (2008). A collaborative immersion approach to evaluation capacity building. *American Journal of Evaluation. 29*(3), 358–368.

Kelly-Woessner, A. (2011, February 13). The great assessment diversion. *Chronicle of Higher Education*. Retrieved from http://chronicle.com/article/The-Great-Assessment-Diversion/126347/

Kezar, A., & Maxey, D. (2014). *Student outcomes assessment among the new non-tenure-track faculty majority*. Champaign, IL: National Institute for Learning Outcomes Assessment.

King, J. A., & Volkov, B. (2005). A framework for building evaluation capacity based on the experiences of three organizations. *CURA Reporter. 35*(3), 10–16.

Labin, S. N., Duffy, J. L., Meyers, D. C., Wandersman, A., & Lesesne, C. A. (2012). A research synthesis of the evaluation capacity building literature. *American Journal of Evaluation. 33*(3), 307–338.

Leviton, L. C. (2014). Some underexamined aspects of evaluation capacity building. *American Journal of Evaluation. 35*(1), 90–94.

Patton, M. Q. (2008). *Utilization-focused evaluation* (4th ed.). Thousand Oaks, CA: Sage.

Preskill, H. (2014). Now for the hard stuff: Next steps in ECB research and practice. *American Journal of Evaluation. 35*(1), 116–119.

Preskill, H., & Boyle, S. (2008). A multidisciplinary model of evaluation capacity building. *American Journal of Evaluation. 29*(4), 443–459.

Provezis, S. (2010). *Regional accreditation and student learning outcomes: Mapping the territory*. Champaign, IL: National Institute for Learning Outcomes Assessment.

Satterlund, T. D., Treiber, J., Kipke, R., Kwon, N., & Cassady, D. (2013). Accommodating diverse clients' needs in evaluation capacity building: A case study of the Tobacco Control Evaluation Center. *Evaluation and Program Planning. 36*(1), 49–55.

Suarez-Balcazar, Y., & Taylor-Ritzler, T. (2014). Moving from science to practice in evaluation capacity building. *American Journal of Evaluation. 35*(1), 95–99.

Tagg, J. (2012). Why does the faculty resist change? *Change: The Magazine of Higher Learning. 44*(1), 6–15.

Taylor-Ritzler, T., Suarez-Balcazar, Y., Garcia-Iriarte, E., Henry, D. B., & Balcazar, F. E. (2013). Understanding and measuring evaluation capacity: A model and instrument validation study. *American Journal of Evaluation. 34*(2), 190–206.

MONICA STITT-BERGH *is an associate specialist of assessment at the University of Hawai'i at Mānoa.*

NEW DIRECTIONS FOR EVALUATION • DOI: 10.1002/ev

Tesch, A. (2016). Implementing pre-post test designs in higher education evaluations. In W. H. Rickards, & M. Stitt-Bergh (Eds.), *Evaluating student learning in higher education: Beyond the public rhetoric. New Directions for Evaluation, 151*, 85–96.

6

Implementing Pre-Post Test Designs in Higher Education Evaluations

Aaron Tesch

Abstract

This chapter outlines the implementation of a pilot project to evaluate courses and an education program with pre-post designs in an undergraduate psychology program. This plan of evaluation incorporates a variety of pre-post test designs to measure the change in student performance across different contexts—including traditional and online courses—rather than rely solely on outcome measures without controls as is common in higher education evaluation. In addition to building on the essential value of this design, this chapter examines a largely faculty-directed evaluation program, which examines the need for expertise in instrument development and pedagogical scholarship, and demonstrates the importance of administrative support. © 2016 Wiley Periodicals, Inc., and the American Evaluation Association.

In the recently published, bestselling book, *The Signal and the Noise*, Nate Silver describes how probabilistic prediction of events is possible, if you have enough data. One example is major league baseball, which has a quantitative database of many of the relevant events that took place in regulation games for the past 100 years (Silver, 2012). You can understand a lot about baseball players by looking at these data, and this information can guide successful interventions to help players reach their full game playing potential (Silver, 2012). Evaluating performance is not only a powerful predictive tool; it can also help guide improvements in interventions for all kinds of disciplines. College educators should take this as a lesson in data management and strive to gather high-quality data that can guide interventions to improve instruction.

Before we can understand anything of merit in the realm of higher education—Silver might suggest—we must first develop data-gathering strategies of similar quality and quantity to those used in baseball. Efforts to measure educational performance are often focused only on performance outcomes, that is, tests given at graduation or comparisons with previous cohorts. For example, program accreditation and student assessments tend to focus solely on performance outcome measures without appropriate controls (Lubinescu, Ratcliff, & Gaffney, 2001). These outcome measures are used, often, as the main measure to determine program effectiveness, although some attempts to measure change in performance have been made (Arum & Roksa, 2011; Liu, 2011). Even studies that try to measure improvement, rather than rely solely on outcomes without controls, often compare cohorts instead of individual students against themselves (Liu, 2011). This practice can indeed control for many variables and is logistically relatively easy. However, cohort studies are subject to misinterpretation when the context of the cohorts is ignored or simply not known (Merrow, Mangini, & Fournelle, 2013). For example, an instructor with highly disadvantaged students may not get credit for the progress a student makes because the comparison cohort, or lack of comparison, does not control for the unique challenges specific students faced.

It is admirable that assessment programs seek to promote better educational practices by using objective data; however, the use of absolute performance outcomes or inappropriate cohort comparisons, rather than individual measures of improvement, distorts the measure of individual student learning during a course or program. These conventions jeopardize the ultimate goal of improving educational practices, because it is not known if any differences are because of the quality of the program, course, or uncontrolled factors. An excellent instructor with the best teaching methodology possible and a supportive administration might still have students who seem to fare relatively poorly compared to bad controls or even show little improvement when compared to unequal cohorts. However, if the measure of quality was based on how much an individual student improved their performance over the time they had with the instructor, credit for that instruction could be more precisely allocated. If change in individual performance during the time the instructor taught the student was the standard educational measure of quality, the student would be his/her own control group, and only then could different instruction/program methodologies be compared fairly. This robust approach helps address general program effects while also being adaptable for studies of specific instructional interventions, such as online learning.

What follows is an account of how one group of educators and administrators set up a higher education evaluation system wherein individual

NEW DIRECTIONS FOR EVALUATION • DOI: 10.1002/ev

student improvement data were collected to inform pedagogical improvements at both the course and program level. These working relationships—and how they emerged over the course of the project—became the focus of learning from this experience; there is more attention to these structural characteristics than the precise results in order to emphasize the developing nature of practice.

Academic Setting

In the fall of 2012, the administration at the University of Arizona South campus (UAS) commissioned a group of faculty to develop coherent program evaluation methods. This campus has a home base in the town of Sierra Vista, Arizona, which lies south of Tucson and is close to the Mexican border. The south campus is a unique blend of a branch campus and outreach program for the main University of Arizona campus in Tucson, Arizona. However, UAS students and courses are taught online and face to face at many southern Arizona locations, including at campuses in and around the main campus' hometown of Tucson (University of Arizona South, 2012). The programs at UAS are also required to limit their offerings to upper-division courses, that is, junior- and senior-level undergraduate courses, because of mutually beneficial agreements with local community colleges.

Broad Mission

Creating evaluation policies and methods for an entire campus, even a small one like UAS, is not a small task. The faculty group—the evaluation team—decided that the best way to introduce a new evaluation paradigm is to create a few program-level evaluations that represent different types of programs the campus offers. Three programs were chosen for this pilot project. The first program was picked because of its status as a joint program that shares all the same criteria and regulations as its counterpart on the main campus in Tucson. The second program was picked because it represents a unique UAS program that has no counterpart on the main campus. The third program was picked because it is a master's level program and therefore focuses on a different population (UAS students only).

As we corrected the inevitable problems that arose as the evaluation procedures were introduced, it was hoped we would refine the procedures enough so other departments would have a strong template to effectively implement their own program evaluations. The pilot program for evaluation procedures for the UAS psychology program was picked because it has a counterpart on the main campus, and it is the focus of this chapter. The development of an evaluation strategy was particularly important for the UAS Psychology Department because it coincided with the introduction of a fully online option for students in this program.

NEW DIRECTIONS FOR EVALUATION • DOI: 10.1002/ev

The addition of a new mode of teaching pushed us to develop assessment plans for both our newly created online courses and the program as a whole—a frequently emerging practice as campuses seek broader student populations. These assessments were designed to give us a view on how the courses and program could be improved. By looking at both levels, we hoped to synchronize adjustments to our overall program with changes at the class level.

Course-Level Evaluations

The goal to improve our courses through the collection and analysis of well-controlled data was a good place to start because a course's curriculum is easier to manage than a whole program. The introduction of many new online courses for the new fully online program also made it a good time to build assessments into the fabric of these courses. The assessment of individual courses also allowed us to test specific instructional techniques. It should also be mentioned that because new courses are taught every semester, the testing of innovations and refinement of existing instructional techniques could be improved on a much shorter time scale than program-level evaluations. We used a pre-post test design with control and experimental group comparisons to ingrain the philosophy of looking at individual improvements. First, new grading techniques were tested and refined in a biopsychology course. Second, differences in teaching environment were tested in a pair of psychology of happiness courses. This adaptability allowed for a kind of metaevaluation during implementation, deepening the ability over time to use evaluation effectively.

Innovations in Grading Techniques: The Biopsychology Course

Research on learning and motivation describes two learning mindsets: growth and fixed (Dweck, 2006). Students with a fixed mindset focus on grades, cheat more often, and do not strive to do better because they do not think they can (Dweck, 2006). It is desirable for teachers to instill interest in a subject as well as understanding by encouraging a focus on the mastery of the subject, rather than students' performance at any given time during the course. Students with a growth mindset have more focus on their effort and understanding and are more likely to persist when learning becomes challenging (Dweck, 2006). However, traditional grading schemes may unintentionally foster a fixed mindset by awarding points only for a few high-stakes assignments and not giving opportunities to improve grades/performance.

In order to foster a growth mindset in our students, we tested different grading schemes in different sections of the biopsychology course (Tesch & Lunsford, 2013): a control group that used a conventional set of graded quizzes and a mastery group in which students could retake quizzes to deepen their knowledge. A pretest posttest design was also used to ensure that any difference found between these groups was a result of our grading schemes, rather than individual variables we could not control for, that is, the timing of class enrollment. Because our sample size was relatively small, we used the more powerful within-subject design. Using a traditional grading scheme where students had only one attempt to demonstrate their knowledge of each unit provided a useful control. Having a good control was the only way to know how our new grading system performed in relation to typical single attempt grading practices.

The first step we took was to split up the course material into manageable units and set up tests for students' understanding of each unit. Breaking learning into shorter segments, that is, distributed practice, increases retention (Baddeley & Longman, 1978; Ebbinghaus, Ruger, & Bussenius, 1913). We also did not want students to cram for a few high-stakes tests and wanted to encourage a sense of temporal coherence in the course, so reasonable deadlines, about one unit per week, were set for the completion of each unit quiz. These policies were meant to create an effective environment for memorization of material by chunking information into manageable units and distributing learning of the material (Mathy & Feldman, 2012; Roediger, 2013).

Students in the control with the traditional grading scheme took each quiz once. Students in the treatment with the mastery-grading scheme could retake quizzes. The first mastery-grading scheme applied was to require at least a 90% score on a unit quiz before moving on. Grades were based on the number of units that were mastered, rather than the score on any particular quiz or assignment. For example, to get an A, students had to get at least a 90% on all of the units and on all of the assignments. Students in this mastery section were given as many quiz attempts as they wanted to master the material. Each quiz was generated by randomly selecting quiz questions from a pool of unit-related questions to discourage rote memorization of the quiz questions and their answers.

The students in both groups took an ungraded diagnostic test based on the course content at the beginning of the class and again at the midpoint. According to student feedback on the formative comparison of the mastery and traditional schemes, students liked the mastery option better. Students were given a chance to switch grading schemes at the midpoint of the course, and most in the traditional grading scheme switched. However, many students in the mastery grading system kept retaking the quizzes without studying the material before their next quiz attempt. They would do this perseverative ritual until they earned the grade required for mastery. These results might not have been a problem if they were actually retaining the information, but a comparison of the course pretest scores with ungraded midterm posttest scores indicated that the mastery-graded students did not improve their content knowledge, whereas the students graded under the traditional process improved at significantly higher levels (Tesch & Lundsford, 2013).

In the subsequent semesters, the quiz grades were averaged to make it clear that each quiz attempt should be taken seriously and study of content would be rewarded with better grades. When quiz scores were averaged, however, students rarely took additional quiz attempts, presumably because they were scared their grades would worsen. Therefore, they did not benefit from additional effort by being rewarded with better grades. Our current policy in this course is to use the mastery grading scheme and average quiz scores but have a "final" attempt that replaces the averaged quiz score if the student proves he/she learned the material. This grading system is not perfect, but it seems to have encouraged more reflection on the material than either the traditional "one shot is all you get" or the "try all you want" mastery grading system.

As is typically the case with uncontrolled enrollment processes, there were inherent complexities in the student groupings and characteristics that complicated the analyses. For example, students who were more excited about the course might have registered earlier and might have filled up the first course section. We also give preference to students enrolled in UA South versus UA Main (and seniors) and this might have skewed our samples in unpredictable ways. By using the pre-post comparison group design, we provided a more precise picture of student development under the different conditions and better information with which analyze the impact of the different grading schemes.

Different Teaching Environments: The Psychology of Happiness Course

Another course-level evaluation where we used a pretest posttest design was in a comparison of online versus face-to-face learning environments. Previous studies that compared online to face-to-face learning had mixed findings, suggesting that the effectiveness of online learning depends on an interaction between both learning environment and pedagogy (Tallent-Runnels et al., 2006). Interest in mastery education and online learning is on the rise because of its potential to increase accessibility and decrease the price of a college education (Parry, 2011). Here again, we used an ungraded diagnostic test of content knowledge at the course beginning and midpoint for both groups of students. In our study, no significant differences in student learning of content were discovered between the online section and face-to-face section using this approach; however, both groups showed significant learning between beginning and midterm (Tesch & Lunsford, 2013).

In terms of mastery learning—and the theoretical concerns in the original evaluation study—the students in both formats were allowed to write supplemental essays analyzing mistakes in their unit quizzes. Students in both platforms were generally enthusiastic, each student completing an average of three essays to deepen their learning. Here again, there were no evident differences in learning in relation to the course platform, but the quality of the student experience provided evidence for further use of this technique and related inquiry.

By using proper controls in this course we were able to see whether the platform—that is, online versus face to face—was truly a factor in student learning. The general lack of proper controls in other settings suggests differences in environment may be less important than other pedagogical concerns, that is, assignments, projects, and grading. Specifically, this use of a diagnostic assessment provides a basis for monitoring learning so that it is possible to more sharply evaluate pedagogical effects including those that are technology based.

Program-Level Evaluation

These small course-level successes encouraged our faculty group to expand our scope and create a plan to apply pre-post test designs to our program assessment. This pre-post model could serve as a standard expansion of assessing a program's strengths and weaknesses and as a case study for the introduction of a fully online option into an existing program. Because of the unique circumstances of our program, we are not endorsing any particular program evaluation procedures at other institutions. Instead, this case's successes and failures can serve as a useful model on how to develop evaluation procedures for other unique programs.

Seeking an Assessment Structure

The first step was to meet with the University of Arizona's Office of Instruction and Assessment. They suggested creating, or adapting, expected learning outcomes (ELOs) for the program using the main campus department's ELOs and/or from national psychology organizations like the American Psychological Association (APA). This might seem extremely basic advice, but it was nice to have some guidance to overcome the current, inadequate procedures. We found that the ELOs posted for our sister program on the main campus were very good. We also discovered that the sister program ELOs were adapted from recommendations generated by one of our national professional associations (i.e., APA). Therefore, by simply observing what others were doing we saved a great deal of work in identifying the topics that defined the goals of our program.

Defining Our ELOs

The ELOs that we gathered were interpreted in a way that could be measured. For example, the APA lists Knowledge Base of Psychology as a goal, which implies that they expect students to gain this knowledge, but we spelled out these assumptions using action words as described by Bloom's Taxonomy, so there would not be any confusion about our goals

(Committee of College and University Examiners, 1956; Pusateri, Halonen, Hill, & McCarthy, 2009). The ELOs adapted from the APA recommendations consisted of the following: (a) Demonstrate a Basic Knowledge Base of Psychology, (b) Identify Values in Psychology, (c) Describe Research Methods used in Psychology, (d) Practice Applications of Psychology, (e) Apply Information and Technological Tools, (f) Discover Communication Skills, (g) Demonstrate Literacy, (h) Show Sociocultural and International Awareness, (i) Construct Evidence of Personal Development, (j) Prepare Career Planning and Development, and (k) Discover Critical Thinking Skills in Psychology. For each of these ELOs a plan was devised to gather data about how the program improved individual outcomes. How we measured these ELOs is described in more detail next.

Defining Our Measurements

For each of the learning outcomes a measurement was devised to collect data on the progress of our students.

Core Psychology Knowledge Assessment. In order to provide a broad-based education in psychology, both departments at the University of Arizona require students to take courses from three subfields of psychology: clinical, social, and cognitive. Our evaluation process sought to incorporate this broad-based program structure into our program evaluation. The main campus department developed a psychology knowledge exam that they give to graduating seniors to measure learning outcomes. This test provides a way to measure psychological knowledge at a basic level, that is, students who passed their courses should be able to answer these questions. In the branch campus department, we decided to take this approach one step further and also test junior-level psychology students that were entering our program at UAS to be able to control for the diversity of their previous educational backgrounds. Our curriculum requires students to become aware of the sociocultural world and these questions help test for that awareness.

Best of Critical Thinking Assessment (BOCA). One outcome that is a priority for our department, other UAS departments, and our counterparts on the main campus, based on recommendations from the APA, is for students to discover critical thinking skills (Pusateri et al., 2009; UAS, 2014). However, when we started to research ways to measure critical thinking we found a large body of research with no universal standards, or tests, for this highly important factor. In lieu of a universal assessment, we created our own critical thinking test, the Best of Critical Thinking Assessment (BOCA), using examples from critical thinking sample questions that we gathered from many different critical thinking tests. By using these archetypical critical thinking questions, we hoped to generate a valid measure of critical thinking.

Testing the Validity of the BOCA. To verify that our critical thinking questions were truly measuring a general critical thinking ability, a pilot study was conducted using a sample of students at the University of Arizona. This pilot study was conducted during the 2011–2012 school year. We recruited 295 students. These students were asked to take the BOCA, either at the beginning or end of their course. They were informed that this test was being used to make improvements to the curriculum and given an opportunity to take it anonymously by clicking on a link provided on the course website. Some caution is required in interpreting these data, but the analysis was limited to within subject comparisons and used only to determine how much individual questions were related.

A Spearman correlation matrix showed that the answers to these questions trended as positively correlated with each other with a few exceptions. A principal component analysis was also done to get a clearer understanding of this data and visualized using the biplot() function in R. This analysis showed there were roughly three factors that could be extracted from the set of questions. However, most of the BOCA questions were answered in a way that trended together. This finding suggests that the BOCA does not measure a clear single factor that we can call critical thinking but most of these submeasures pointed in a similar direction suggesting these measures are at least tangentially related. Thus we can put some weight into student performance on the BOCA as a way of measuring their general critical thinking ability and look at their specific answers to determine strengths in different kinds of critical thinking.

The fall 2013 incoming class of psychology students at UAS also took the BOCA. Another principal component analysis showed similar results. In the future, we will focus on expected improvements in the ability to think critically over the course of our academic program. Two equivalent versions of the BOCA should be given to incoming and outgoing UAS psychology students so we can determine if their critical thinking ability improves during the program. These assessments will also provide a baseline for finding expected changes in critical thinking ability, and they can be compared to future cohorts to assess the effects of changes to the program, that is, new online options for students.

Bookend Courses. The psychology program at UAS requires the completion of basic research methodology courses, that is, statistics and research methods, for entrance into the program. However, students joining our program have very diverse academic backgrounds, and because many of our courses are taught online, we wanted to engender a sense of community from the beginning of their academic careers. To create this sense of community and to get at least a qualitative pre-post measurement of five of our ELOs, we created two highly recommended courses that bookend our students' experience within our program. Because we had to align our requirements with the other University of Arizona psychology departments, we could recommend/encourage the taking of only these two courses. The first bookend course reviews basic concepts in the field and provides a chance for students in the incoming cohort to get to know each other.

NEW DIRECTIONS FOR EVALUATION • DOI: 10.1002/ev

The second bookend course is taught at the end of our students' experience and provides ways to apply everything students have learned during the program to their own lives. By completing these courses a student is evaluated on his or her incoming and outgoing basic knowledge of psychological concepts, identification of psychological values, description of research methods, practice in the application of psychology in the real world, technological proficiency, ability to communicate, and educational literacy.

The students' technological proficiency is tested in both courses because they both include requirements to use technological tools common in the field of psychology, that is, use of statistical software (R, Excel, or SPSS) and presentation software (PowerPoint, YouTube, or Panopto). A student's ability to apply information and technological tools can be measured by the quality of these assignments and their improvement in technological ability can be estimated by comparing their performance in similar assignments used in both bookends courses.

One of the most important skills acquired during college is the ability to communicate ideas to others. Measuring this skill is difficult, but as with many of our other ELOs we have developed a pair of assignments that track students' improvements in communication. Our bookend courses offer a structured way of doing this by using comparable assignments at the beginning and end of our program. In both bookend courses, students are asked to create presentations that are shared with the other students in the course. By comparing the quality of these presentations, we are able to observe improvements in their communication skills.

College students are also required to read and understand psychological writing. To measure improvements in literacy during the time they attend our program, again, we used our bookend courses as the standard for demonstrating literacy. Both bookend courses require reading and comprehension of complex ideas, so we test how quickly students acquired this knowledge by looking at how many quiz attempts they take in each course, and by looking at the quality of their last quiz attempt to measure the extent of their grasp of the concepts that were tested. As their psychological literacy improved, we expected to see less of a struggle in the second bookend course than in the first.

Discussion

This chapter encourages investigating change using pre-post test comparison group designs, rather than using posttest-only outcome measures to determine the quality of a course or program. This methodology will allow for more fine tuning of improvements because it increases the measurement of what the course or program can influence, reducing the substantial demographic error that plagues much of educational assessment. Developing and implementing course evaluations that truly take into account the starting

NEW DIRECTIONS FOR EVALUATION • DOI: 10.1002/ev

point of students' knowledge and skills in the field of educational evaluation are rare. Ours was a largely faculty-directed activity and one that involved extensive reflection on the learning principles and intended outcomes in the program as well as technical expertise in instrument development and use and pedagogical innovations. In full implementation, it will be necessary to randomize conditions to appropriately control validity threats, but the current work has been a chance to demonstrate feasibility of the more controlled comparison and build credibility among the faculty for using such an approach.

It should also be noted that the heads of our program were active and willing participants in the development of this evaluation process, and the alignment of process and goals was an important part of its implementation. The lack of buy-in is one of the most important parts of this process. For example, one of the biggest reasons that the presecondary reforms, No Child Left Behind and Race to the Top, were not embraced is that they did not have the buy-in from the teachers (Harjunen, 2009). The evaluations used in these reforms did not generally use appropriate controls for measuring improvements in student achievement at a useful level for classroom instruction.

Teachers, schools, and districts are often judged by outcome measure comparisons of student test scores, and state grade-level standards and comparisons are often used as the main measure to determine teacher, school, and administrator effectiveness (Carey & Manwaring, 2011; Merrow et al., 2013; Quaid, 2009). Other presecondary reform policies focused on how much the student scores had changed from previous cohorts and not individual improvement (Merrow et al., 2013). Future reforms should first create buy-in from all stakeholders before implementation of reforms because without them reforms will fail (Harjunen, 2009).

Without buy-in from the administration, advisors, teachers, and students, our program evaluation plan was not as successful as our course reforms. Few students chose to take the second bookend course or take the exit surveys, that is, BOCA/core psychology assessment, and therefore, the first set of data was too sparse to analyze or draw conclusions from it. Despite these struggles, the participating instructors valued the opportunity to observe individual performance during the courses and the processes have increased the readiness for future collaboration. The need for program or course evaluation using a clear empirical foundation is critical to implementing reforms, but this process should be uniquely tailored to the educational environment. We encourage others to go through their own process to discover what will work for their own unique educational programs and students, with local validation for data collection procedures and attention to assessed changes in learning. When we say a program worked, we want to be able to talk about individual changes in students' performance that were measured over the course of the class or program. To rely on outcome measures alone misses at least half of their story and cannot really be compared to other programs because these students did not go to those other programs.

References

Arum, R., & Roksa, J. (2011). *Academically adrift: Limited learning on college campuses.* Chicago, IL: University of Chicago Press.

Baddeley, A. D., & Longman, D. J. A. (1978). The influence of length and frequency of training sessions on the rate of learning to type. *Ergonomics. 21*(8), 627–635.

Carey, K., & Manwaring, R. (2011). *Growth models and accountability: A recipe for remaking ESEA* (Education Sector Reports). Washington, DC: Education Sector. Retrieved from http://educationpolicy.air.org/sites/default/files/publications/GrowthModelsAnd Accountability_Release%20.pdf

Committee of College and University Examiners. (1956). *Taxonomy of educational objectives* (Vol. 1). New York, NY: David McKay.

Dweck, C. (2006). *Mindset: The new psychology of success.* New York, NY: Random House.

Ebbinghaus, H., Ruger, H. A., & Bussenius, C. E. (1913). *Memory: A contribution to experimental psychology.* New York, NY: Dover.

Harjunen, E. (2009). How do teachers view their own pedagogical authority? *Teachers and Teaching: Theory and Practice. 15*(1), 109–129.

Liu, O. L. (2011). Value-added assessment in higher education: A comparison of two methods. *Higher Education. 61*(4), 445–461.

Lubinescu, E. S., Ratcliff, J. L., & Gaffney, M. A. (2001). Two continuums collide: Accreditation and assessment. *New Directions for Higher Education: No. 113. How accreditation influences assessment* (pp. 5–21). San Francisco, CA: Jossey-Bass.

Mathy, F., & Feldman, J. (2012). What's magic about magic numbers? Chunking and data compression in short-term memory. *Cognition. 122*(3), 346–362.

Merrow, J. (Correspondent), Mangini, T., & Fournelle, C. (Directors). (2013). The education of Michelle Rhee [Television series episode]. In M. Joseloff (Producer), *Frontline.* Arlington, VA: Public Broadcasting Service.

Parry, M. (2011, August 31). Online education is everywhere. What's the next big thing? *Chronicle of Higher Education.* Retrieved from http://chronicle.com/blogs/ wiredcampus/online-education-is-everywhere-whats-the-next-big-thing/32898

Pusateri, T., Halonen, J., Hill, B., & McCarthy, M. (2009). *The assessment cyberguide for learning goals and outcomes.* Washington, DC: American Psychological Association Education Directorate.

Quaid, L. (2009). Obama education plan speech: Stricter standards, charter schools, merit pay. *Huffington Post.* Retrieved from http://www.huffingtonpost.com

Roediger, H. L. (2013). Applying cognitive psychology to education translational educational science. *Psychological Science in the Public Interest. 14*(1), 1–3.

Silver, N. (2012). *The signal and the noise: Why so many predictions fail—but some don't.* New York, NY: Penguin Press.

Tallent-Runnels, M. K., Thomas, J. A., Lan, W. Y., Cooper, S., Ahern, T. C., Shaw, S. M., & Liu, X. (2006). Teaching courses online: A review of the research. *Review of Educational Research. 76*(1), 93–135.

Tesch, A. D., & Lunsford, L. (2013, April). *An analysis of course innovations in grading and assignments that emphasize learning: Biopsychology and psychology of happiness.* Poster session presented at the meeting of the Western Psychological Association, Reno, NV.

University of Arizona South (UAS) Admissions. (2012). *"Welcome"* [Brochure]. Sierra Vista, AZ. Retrieved from http://uas.arizona.edu/admissions

AARON TESCH is a senior lecturer at the University of Arizona South.

Secolsky, C., Sng, C., Wentland, E., & Smith III, D. L. (2016). Assessment of student learning outcomes: Evaluator and client communication. In W. H. Rickards & M. Stitt-Bergh (Eds.), *Evaluating student learning in higher education: Beyond the public rhetoric. New Directions for Evaluation, 151*, 97–107.

7

Assessment of Student Learning Outcomes: Evaluator and Client Communication

Charles Secolsky, Clarice Sng, Ellen Wentland, Dwight L. Smith III

Abstract

Revolving around threats to internal validity, several of which are new, this chapter characterizes how evaluators might want to communicate with stakeholders on problems of student learning outcomes assessment. Seven scenarios from our experience are developed for the evaluator to consider, with each one presenting a different challenge working with faculty members in higher education. Test scores, rubrics, and embedded questions suggest the need for more effective communication when stakeholders need methodological guidance. It is very important for evaluators to work with stakeholders from the beginning of the assessment process to avoid potential pitfalls and erroneous interpretations of data. © 2016 Wiley Periodicals, Inc., and the American Evaluation Association.

I nstitutions of higher education commonly employ individuals with research and evaluation backgrounds to serve as assessment directors or coordinators to provide structure and expertise to faculty members involved in student learning outcomes assessment processes. Functions encompassed in that role typically include working with faculty to (a) articulate learning outcomes; (b) identify student products that would reflect progress on those outcomes; (c) develop processes to collect and evaluate student products using appropriate methods and tools; and (c) facilitate interpretation and use of assessment results for program improvement, a process referred to as "closing the loop."

These assessment directors or coordinators may have various institutional titles, and additional responsibilities but are referred to in this chapter collectively as "evaluators."

With a heightened national focus on learning assessment in higher education, and with an increased emphasis by regional accrediting agencies on institutions developing well-designed and ongoing learning outcomes assessment processes, the role of an evaluator is critical to higher education institutions' self-assessment and self-improvement efforts. For an evaluator to be effective, he/she has to build and maintain an ongoing relationship with faculty members based on mutual trust and respect. It is a relationship patiently built on continuous, transparent, open, considerate feedback and communication with a sincere desire to help faculty do their work better. A good start is for faculty and evaluator to acknowledge and respect each other's expertise and domain: the faculty in the areas of subject matter and student behavior and the evaluator in the areas of evaluation and assessment.

From the faculty perspective, one can think of a number of reasons why some would not like to get involved in student learning outcomes assessment. First and foremost is the fear of being evaluated. According to Donaldson, Gooler, and Scriven (2002), the fear of receiving a negative evaluation is "probably inherent to being human," feeling threatened by the evaluator and ambivalent about the evaluation process. The consequences of such anxieties, they suggest, can be numerous: challenging the validity of evaluation results, lack of cooperation by key stakeholders and decision makers (e.g., faculty), difficulty in obtaining access to required information, dissatisfaction with program evaluation. One critical task of the evaluator is to communicate to faculty in words and actions that the focus of learning outcomes assessment is on what students are learning and in finding ways to improve upon that learning, rather than on the performance of individual faculty members.

A second possible reason for faculty members not wanting to get involved in student learning outcomes assessment is that faculty members are concerned that their role as subject matter and student experts may be usurped by the often nonfaculty evaluator. The enormous demand on faculty time, which outcomes assessment work requires, becomes a third obstacle to a successful assessment program.

Even in cases where there is a strong vested interest in learning outcomes assessment for a particular program, evaluators can find themselves working with faculty who may not possess an adequate understanding of how to develop an effective learning outcomes process, one that can serve both faculty and student needs; they may also lack experience in working with evaluators and how best to leverage evaluators' expertise for program improvement.

At heart is a need for regular, positive, and constructive communication between the evaluator and faculty members. Social psychologists have come onto the evaluation scene of late with theories about communication and persuasive and collaborative leadership to engage program leaders. For example, Campbell and McGrath (2011), analyzing communication between evaluators and stakeholders, state, "Involving key stakeholders in evaluation decision making from the beginning will increase primary intended use by primary intended users" (p. 357)—in this context, faculty members involved in assessment work. Thus, in assessment contexts, evaluators should not independently make decisions for a program or present themselves as experts or authorities. Rather, evaluators must be perceived as partners with faculty and recognize that everyone involved has useful information to contribute. This approach facilitates communication and increases the likelihood of the use of assessment results to inform action and improve student learning. Mark, Donaldson, and Campbell's 2011 volume on social psychology and evaluation demonstrates the importance of communication, persuasion and commitment in improving assessment processes, introducing interventions, and navigating problems like erroneous use of statistical tests. (See also Ajzen, 2011.)

Our focus is on a key element in successful program evaluations, namely, communication, or the effective sharing of information among the parties involved. In this chapter, we describe some of our experiences with faculty, followed by an analysis of those experiences, and also share our reflections on how delicate situations might be negotiated while still delivering feedback and communicating results in a sensitive and respectful manner.

Seven examples are outlined separately and analyzed. Some of these illustrate certain of Campbell and Stanley's (1963) threats to internal validity for quantitative research designs—for example, regression to the mean, which can be applied to student learning outcomes in higher education. Some applications involved large testing companies, university and community college settings, and state agencies; others individual programs. We bring perspectives from both the insiders' and external reviewers' side of the situation.

The Ceiling Effect: "My Whole Class Received Scores of 100"

In some evaluations of student learning outcomes in higher education, assessment is carried out to measure change before and after an intervention. A ceiling effect occurs when there is very little or no room for improvement in student scores because a group of students has attained the highest level of scores possible. Possible explanations for all students obtaining maximum or near-maximum scores include the following:

- All students have mastered the material achieving the targeted outcomes.
- The learning outcome is insufficiently articulated and lacks significant facets.

NEW DIRECTIONS FOR EVALUATION • DOI: 10.1002/ev

- The assessment method (e.g., a rubric or examination) has not been sufficiently developed and therefore fails, on the criterion side, to address all of the important components of the outcome or, on the standards side, to sufficiently differentiate levels of performance.
- Concern about course evaluation leads to an easy test.

To address the first of these points, the evaluator might consult privately with the senior faculty member; this could lead to a deeper discussion of high-impact pedagogies (cf., Kuh, 2010; the Community College Survey of Student Engagement; Wieman, 2015). Senior faculty members may then be encouraged to share techniques and approaches with other faculty, an invitation which is typically very well received by all.

Involvement with faculty from the beginning and throughout the assessment process can help to address the second and third points. Evaluators can work with faculty to parse out the main facets or elements in the outcomes being assessed. Articulating these elements can help in the development or selection of an appropriate rubric, including all of the elements as criteria, possibly with assigned weights. Next, standards for rating can be elaborated to adequately capture the different levels of each criterion.

When the evaluator and faculty work together on steps such as these, important learning opportunities present themselves. Taking time to articulate the components of a learning outcome may prompt increased instructional attention to those components and to designing assignments that emphasize them. Faculty involvement in the selection or development of appropriate rubrics represents an opportunity for faculty to clarify their expectations regarding student performance. When these rubrics are then shared with students, which many evaluators encourage, faculty report that students appreciate having been provided with the rubric-borne assignment expectations. The grading process is facilitated, and students are more likely to consider assigned grades to be fair, given the transparency that the rubrics provide, potentially contributing to positive course evaluations—the fourth explanatory point. For whatever reason, an "easy" assessment for either pretest or posttest in the outcomes assessment loop decreases the ability to assess true change as a result of an intervention.

Gain Scores Produced from Pre-Post Assessments Are Internally Valid: Regression to the Mean

Gain scores have become the focus of national conversation in higher education in the not too distant past (U.S. Department of Education, 2006) and with the publication of *Academically Adrift: Limited Learning on College Campuses* (Arum & Roksa, 2011). The Spellings Commission report recommended value-added approaches in higher education assessment of student achievement at the institutional level—with higher educational achievement assessed with respect to some baseline of achievement to show growth as a result of an intervention, that is, the higher educational experience it-self. One potential problem if pretest scores are not factored into the analysis is that institutions starting off with high-achieving students cannot demon-strate significant improvement or value added to the same extent as institu-tions with students starting out with lower achieving students. Arum and Roksa (2011) attempted to demonstrate that student gains in domains like critical thinking have been surprisingly lower than what was previously believed. Additionally, critics of value added (Banta & Pike, 2007) and a replication of the *Academically Adrift* study (Pascarella, Blaich, Martin, & Hanson, 2011) state that a number of limitations emerge in terms of not taking into account initial abilities of freshmen and for the study itself for claiming causal inferences without using a control group.

These large-scale studies suggest the complexities facing program di-rectors using pretest-posttest differences to assess gains at their individual institutions. They may elect to report gain, difference, or change scores to indicate the extent to which students or other program participants have improved on outcome measures, such as test scores. Program directors may be hasty to produce these scores without adequate analysis of issues in-volved. On a pretest, extreme scores found in large numbers pose a threat to internal validity in the gain scores through regression to the mean. If stu-dents have extreme scores at the upper levels of the ability spectrum on the pretest, the posttest scores will likely show a decrease or a maintenance of high score levels. With extreme scores at the lower end of the ability spec-trum, very large gains are likely to be found on the posttest measure. The evaluator needs to work with the program faculty to assist with interpreting the scores obtained by students.

Item Analysis: "I'm Not Sure We Wrote Good Exam Questions"

Outcomes assessment instruments can take many different forms from embedded exam questions to full-length examinations to rubrics. Faculty may be familiar with constructing instruments such as those that contain true–false or multiple-choice type questions. More likely, however, it is the evaluator and not the faculty member who is knowledgeable about item–test correlations and differential item functioning (DIF) indices for iden-tifying potential item invalidity or item bias disfavoring certain student groups.

Item–test correlations enable the detection of items in which higher ability students (i.e., with high total test scores) miss an item that is am-biguous because of reading too deeply into the question whereas students with lower total test scores respond correctly mostly by guessing. For a po-tentially biased item exhibiting DIF, matched groups of equal ability on the total test scores show differential performance on individual items. Both these features of item analysis make for better instruments through pretest-ing and not scoring unfair items in operational administrations.

NEW DIRECTIONS FOR EVALUATION • DOI: 10.1002/ev

For most faculty members, item analysis and especially DIF analysis may be a daunting task not even seen as necessary by accrediting bodies. Yet, the validity of an assessment hinges on the fairness of the instrument. For this reason, as the outcomes assessment movement continues forward and standards for assessment become more stringent, evaluators unfamiliar with item analysis will have to learn new techniques in assessment and train faculty members in these techniques. This will require even greater communication between evaluators and faculty members. (For information on item analysis and DIF for small samples, the reader is referred to Clauser and Hambleton, 2012.)

Scores Have Gone Up! (and We Tweaked Some of the Items)

At a curriculum committee meeting at a community college, the chairperson of a psychology department presented the results of five administrations of an outcomes assessment instrument using embedded questions. The chairperson pointed out that the increasing scores were part of a trend. He also noted that certain items had been reworded because prior administration of the former version of the test had shown that students could not understand those items. The items were reworded.

However, to interpret the higher scores as showing a favorable trend, after test items have been reworded to make them easier to understand, would be fallacious. In this example, higher scores do not indicate true improvement in student ability over time. It also could be that the items were poorly constructed in the first place.

The evaluator is now faced with the dilemma of whether to correct the chairperson on the spot or speak to him after the curriculum committee meeting. An additional confounding problem is that the other curriculum committee members have been presented with the chairperson's erroneous interpretation. In this example, the participant does not recognize the fallacy of the argument he is making by espousing that both:

- the items have been "tweaked" or made easier for students to get correct answers, and
- scores have increased as part of a trend.

Although evaluators know how to identify mistakes of those who report data on outcomes, the evaluator has to consider when, where and how to correct participants' errors in the evaluation process. Some people would feel more comfortable with being corrected on the spot in an effort to work toward a common goal with the evaluator going forward, but others not. The evaluator needs to pay careful attention to the context.

This situation is one that could be avoided if evaluators are consistently involved with the faculty members as they create assessment tools, such as developing test items. In this situation, the evaluator should be

NEW DIRECTIONS FOR EVALUATION • DOI: 10.1002/ev

working with the department faculty prior to the implementation of an assessment tool to make sure that the tool and its items are valid and reliable. Item "tweaking" may be needed when it is found that items do not "work" properly, but this would also be a joint project. Cautions about interpreting changes in performance following such "tweaking" could be made, along with possible suggestions that would allow for comparisons between the old and new test scores, a suggestion that would likely be welcomed by the faculty as opposed to discarding work that took time and effort. There are a number of equating alternatives that can be considered such as equipercentile and common item linear equating to ensure score comparability across forms (see Kolen & Hendrickson, 2012).

Misaligning Rubric Criteria with What Was Expected of Students to Learn: A Lack of Content Validity for Rubrics

Rubric scores are meant to reflect student abilities/proficiencies vis-a-vis particular learning outcomes in a particular instructional context. But what happens if the rubric evaluates what students have not been taught and there is a misalignment of the rubric in terms of topic coverage? This can occur when faculty use a rubric developed out of the context of their particular course and classroom and then fail to adequately evaluate the suitability of the rubric for their particular instructional situation. Rubrics on a wide variety of topics are readily available on the Web, but before use, they must be carefully analyzed and then perhaps modified to ensure appropriateness. Evaluators can assist faculty in first detailing the important components of the outcome(s) to be assessed and then in locating rubrics that may be suitable to use, with or without modifications, or in developing rubrics to ensure a precise fit. Again, the evaluator must be careful not to damage his/her relationship with the faculty member or program director, but bringing this issue up "after the fact" results in time and effort being wasted, with the residual effects of diminished trust and decreased willingness to cooperate in the future.

The issue here is one of content validity (see Sireci, 2007), which can be applied to rubrics. Content validity is fundamental to all of the methodological concerns discussed in this chapter and should be addressed across the program's student learning outcomes assessment process. But it emerges in a particular fashion in rubric construction; it is advisable for the evaluator to have worked with the faculty members up front as they create or consider the rubrics that they will use, as well as the assessment tools to be included, in relation to the curriculum plan.

We Used a Rubric But Looked Only at Criterion Scores—What About Interrater Reliability?

Grading art work, music projects, and written essays is an example of assessment that either calls for raters who have been trained to adhere to scoring guidelines and measurement goals or for at least two raters to obtain agreement on their ratings. Faculty members serving as program directors often use rubrics in their assessment of student proficiency. However, as Judd, Secolsky, and Allen (2012) determined, if interrater reliability is not taken into consideration, program directors may infer that criterion scores—namely the scores that are the ratings of rubric characteristics—largely determine the variation of ratings, whereas some portion of that variation is actually attributable to a lack of interrater reliability. Criterion scores are the scores having to do with ratings of student work product characteristics, for example, art work receives scores for organization, creativity, and presentation. Evaluators should therefore closely monitor the application of rubrics and work with program directors to develop a process for addressing interrater reliability (e.g., conducting "norming" or "calibration" sessions, establishing common understanding of the criteria and standards, and interpreting student work accordingly). A common approach in writing assessment when there is disagreement between the first two raters is to invite a third rater as an adjudicator. Not only does this evaluator-led approach help ensure that the assessment work leads to valid conclusion and recommendations, but it is also a valuable teaching tool to use with faculty and ideally can carry over to their classroom work. For example, engaging colleagues to be second raters of student work can engender buy-in to the assessment process.

Trying to Get Interventions to Be Successful Without Carefully Developed Plans

Assuming that high-quality usable results are produced from learning outcomes assessment efforts and findings locate program areas in need of improvement, the responsibility of developing a plan to respond to the findings lies with faculty or program managers.

Although there are higher education programs that use assessment results effectively, there are also situations where faculty may not have the experience or know-how to develop and implement a plan to systematically address the findings.

For example, the mathematics department faculty in a community college in the northeast received the results of a test in basic mathematics that showed a large deficiency in student knowledge and skill on the topic of percentages across all levels of mathematics taught at the community college. Probably alarmed, both faculty and the mathematics department chairperson felt the need to quickly address this gap was of paramount importance. In response, the mathematics department instituted a "Percentages Across the Curriculum" plan to help students increase knowledge and skill on the topic of percentages. Initially, it seemed like a reasonable response plan. Postassessment results showed that the response plan did eradicate the deficiency in student knowledge and skill on the topic of percentages across all levels of mathematics taught at the community college, which made it a success. However, postassessment results also now showed that students' knowledge and skill on the topic of rational numbers decreased, likely because of instructional time taken away from rational numbers in remedying deficiencies in percentages.

What can the evaluator do to communicate to program staff that more comprehensive planning is needed for a successful intervention strategy? And how could communication between the evaluator and mathematics faculty for this type of situation—and the revised, but potentially flawed, new curriculum emphasis—have been improved for possibly avoiding this problem?

Discipline-based tools such as the Association of American Colleges and Universities' VALUE rubrics provide outcomes that could can help provide a broad picture of be shared with program faculty. But curriculum mapping of learning outcomes would help address unintended consequences of curricular changes (cf., Uchiyama & Radin, 2009).

Discussion

In a student assessment context, examining these seven concerns with stakeholders in mind leads to a deeper analysis of the challenges for the evaluator. Entanglement with ceiling effects, problems with content validity and rubric misalignment and other misapplications could be addressed through communication between evaluator and faculty member or program director or if the evaluator was treated as an important stakeholder from the beginning. Additionally, when evaluator expertise is combined with faculty subject matter expertise, educators can pursue alternatives for analysis rather than prematurely closing the assessment loop.

Hersey and Blanchard's (1969) model of situational leadership is relevant for rethinking the issues of communication for assessment scenarios like these. They espouse in their theory that one must adapt one's leadership style to that of the collaborating group. That said, communication between the evaluator and faculty member or program director and other technical staff should be at least conciliatory, the evaluator serving as catalyst for alternative methods, helping to develop a "culture of assessment" on a campus.

With respect to the educator role, one approach that evaluators may use is to develop a "training" session, within which various scenarios or real-life cases like those outlined in this chapter are presented to faculty. These cases would all have certain flaws that would compromise assessment results and conclusions. The group would identify exactly what the problems are with the cases presented and discuss how to correct them. These examples would be taken from "other campuses" and would then not be threatening to faculty. This analytic exercise is an opportunity to take up plausible cases that can be engaging, challenging, and entertaining, while also serving to enhance faculty's perceptions and acceptance of the evaluator's expertise. Also, it gives the evaluator the opportunity to appreciate the faculty member's contribution and expertise.

In essence, there exist many fine points in the student learning assessment process that require methodological expertise that the evaluator should have and be able to impart to the faculty member/director. How it is communicated is of the utmost concern to all parties because inappropriate inferences yield misguided interpretations of data and ill-founded recommendations. Regional commissions on higher education in the United States such as the Middle States Commission on Higher Education were initially more concerned with faculty buy-in than the correctness of the methodology used. This is starting to change as methodological correctness is beginning to take hold in the administration of student learning outcomes assessment programs and processes. The result is new opportunities for evaluators to share their expertise, learn from faculty, and ensure a high-quality assessment process that can benefit all stakeholders.

References

Ajzen, I. (2011). Behavioral interventions: Design and evaluation guided by the theory of planned behavior. In M. M. Mark, S. I. Donaldson, & B. Campbell (Eds.), *Social psychology and evaluation* (pp. 74–100). New York, NY: Guilford Press.

Arum, R., & Roksa, J. (2011). *Academically adrift: Limited learning on college campuses.* Chicago, IL: University of Chicago Press.

Banta, T. W., & Pike, G. R. (2007). Revisiting the blind alley of value added. *Assessment Update. 19*(1), 1–2, 14–15.

Campbell, B., & McGrath, A. L. (2011). Where the rubber hits the road: The development of usable middle-range evaluation theories. In M. M. Mark, S. I. Donaldson, & B. Campbell (Eds.), *Social psychology and evaluation* (pp. 346–371). New York, NY: Guilford Press.

Campbell, D. T., & Stanley, J. (1963) *Experimental and quasi-experimental designs for research.* Chicago, IL: Rand-McNally.

Clauser, J. C., & Hambleton, R. K. (2012). Item analysis procedures for classroom assessments in higher education. In C. Secolsky & D. B. Denison (Eds.), *Handbook on measurement, assessment, and evaluation in higher education* (pp. 296–309). New York, NY: Routledge.

Donaldson, S. I., Gooler, L. E., & Scriven, M. (2002). Strategies for managing evaluation anxiety: Toward a psychology of program evaluation. *American Journal of Evaluation. 23*(3), 261–273.

Hersey, P., & Blanchard, K. H. (1969). *Management of organizational behavior: Utilizing human resources.* Englewood Cliffs, NJ: Prentice Hall.

Judd, T. P., Secolsky, C., & Allen, C. (2012, February). *Being confident about results from rubrics.* Champaign, IL: National Institute for Learning Outcomes Assessment, University of Illinois at Urbana-Champaign.

Kolen, M. J., & Hendrickson, A. B. (2012). Scaling, norming, and equating. In C. Secolsky & D. B. Denison (Eds.), *Handbook on measurement, assessment, and evaluation in higher education* (pp. 161–177). New York, NY: Routledge.

Kuh, G. D. (2010). Foreword. In J. E. Brownell & L. E. Swaner (Eds.), *Five high-impact practices: Research on learning outcomes, completion, and quality.* Washington, DC: Association of American Colleges & Universities.

Mark, M. M., Donaldson, S. I., & Campbell, B. (Eds.). (2011). *Social psychology and evaluation*. New York, NY: The Guilford Press.

Pascarella, E. T., Blaich, C., Martin, G. L., & Hanson, J. N. (2011). How robust are the findings of academically adrift? *Change: The Magazine of Higher Learning. 43*(3), 20–24.

Sireci, S. G. (2007). On validity theory and test validation. *Educational Researcher. 36*(8), 477–481.

Uchiyama, K. P., & Radin, J. L. (2009). Curriculum mapping in higher education: A vehicle for collaboration. *Innovations in Higher Education. 33*, 271–280.

U.S. Department of Education. (2006). *A test of leadership: Charting the future of U.S. higher education*. Washington, DC: Author.

Wieman, C. (2015, January-February). A better way to evaluate undergraduate teaching. *Change Magazine*, 7–15.

CHARLES SECOLSKY *specializes in measurement, assessment, and program evaluation at Alternative Assessment Strategies, Inc.*

CLARICE SNG *is the associate director of the office of accreditation and assessment at Teachers College, Columbia University.*

ELLEN WENTLAND *is currently an educational consultant; formerly she was associate dean of educational effectiveness at Northern Essex Community College.*

DWIGHT L. SMITH III *is the vice president for academic affairs at the County College of Morris.*

NEW DIRECTIONS FOR EVALUATION • DOI: 10.1002/ev

Eubanks, D., & Gliem, D. (2016). Recursive validity and authentic outcomes. In W. H. Rickards, & M. Stitt-Bergh (Eds.), *Evaluating student learning in higher education: Beyond the public rhetoric. New Directions for Evaluation, 151,* 109–122.

8

Recursive Validity and Authentic Outcomes

David Eubanks, David Gliem

Abstract

This chapter defines recursive validity as a self-reinforcing loop of observation and judgment, which emphasizes that observation and reporting are most useful when they can be conceptualized by decision makers in such a way as to (a) integrate with their conceptions of reality and (b) be confirmed when actions result in expected outcomes. This approach leads us away from unnecessary abstraction and encourages the testing of predictive validity of proxy measurements. In a full program of research, it also requires an external critique of observational bias to recognize potential false justification. With this framework in place, we apply it to a difficult problem in higher education: how to assess learning outcomes in a way that is convincing to stakeholders. © 2016 Wiley Periodicals, Inc., and the American Evaluation Association.

I n this chapter we develop categories of knowledge and relationships between them to help identify the strengths and weaknesses of evaluation writ large, comprising not just the formal elements, but the impact of reports on actions of stakeholders. This general framework is then applied to the assessment of student learning outcomes in order to give a useful illustrative example. This is timely because learning outcomes are central to the ongoing public discourse on the value and cost of higher education. The public would like to know how to interpret the meaning of a degree and results such as test scores, transcripts, and credentials. A process we call *recursive validity* is intended to steer our internal "realities" toward alignment with the perspective of external stakeholders. As a self-reinforcing loop of observation and judgment that includes actions and consequences outside the university setting, recursive validity emphasizes that observation and reporting should be used by decision makers in such a way as to (a) integrate observations with their conceptions of reality and (b) be confirmed when actions result in expected outcomes.

We start by describing this recursive loop and point to issues that arise when the loop is not complete. The practice of evaluation includes judgments that juxtapose observations, analysis, and context with standards or ideals. Any resulting formal report becomes a kind of bureaucratic reality that we refer to as a *description*. As an example, a course grade given by an instructor is a description, which we denote with brackets, as in [John earned an A in calculus]. Many students will have the same description regardless of their instructor, college, grading standards, or other factor. But this uncertainty is not reflected in the [John earned an A in calculus]. On the contrary, that fact will have perfect reliability among readers of the transcript: everyone will agree that it is an A.

Any evaluative report takes the messy physical universe and produces language: schematically represented here as $\{*\} \rightarrow [\dots]$, where $\{*\}$ is the ineffable stuff that comprises time and space, and the ellipsis stands in for some description resulting from observation. This process, denoted by the arrow, of turning observations into descriptions we call *classification*. The consistency of $\{*\} \rightarrow [\dots]$ classification is usually called reliability. We may then argue about the meaning of the language, but the literal words have nearly complete reliability (and by that virtue have more weight than they might deserve).

If descriptions resulting from evaluation processes are to be of any use, they must be considered by stakeholders when making decisions. This entails a complex human process of integrating professional knowledge, context, goals and costs, politics, and so on into planning. If descriptions are used in this way, we call this process *conceptualization* and denote the newly synthesized conclusion with double brackets. For example, [John has an A in calculus but Bob has only a C- in calculus] $\rightarrow$ [[I should hire John instead of Bob]]. Here the arrow denotes the conceptualization. Because the value judgments we make as individuals are different than mere descriptions, we call the double-bracketed kind a *conception*. The nested brackets help us visualize the internalization of descriptions as they become conceptions. Each of the transitions, from $\{*\}$ to $[\dots]$ and from there to $[[\dots]]$ contains threats to a successful evaluation.

The second transition, from a description $[\dots]$ to its conception $[[\dots]]$, can be problematic. Because descriptions are a highly compressed representation of $\{*\}$, important details may be left out. An example is the enthusiasm in the popular press for *Academically Adrift* (Arum & Roksa, 2011), where we find the argument [normalized pre/posttest scores show little difference] $\rightarrow$ [[college students don't learn anything]]. Bennett and

Figure 8.1. The Recursive Loop from Observation to Action and Back Again

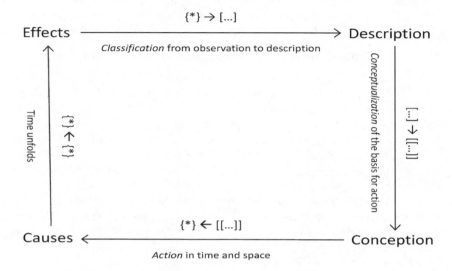

Hacker (2003) call this kind of sleight-of-hand a *mereological fallacy*, where only a fraction of the comprehensive {∗}is observed. Measuring teaching effectiveness of professors by examining the grades they give would be a similar problem. In addition to missing the bigger picture, the trip from [. . .] to [[. . .]] can be distorted by irrationality, such as confirmation bias (for good news) or denial (for bad news). These details matter because stakeholders will inform future actions based on their conceptions [[. . .]], which easily drift out of connection with reality. Some researchers have hypothesized that humans are actually evolved to deceive themselves (Trivers, 2011). These sources of error paint a gloomy picture for any organization that wants to make well-informed decisions and for the evaluators who intend to support that process.

We propose that a reasonable standard for assessing the quality of descriptions and consequent actions is a self-adjusting epistemic loop, shown in schematic form in Figure 8.1. Figure 8.1 adds two new transitions. The first is acting on a conception [[. . .]] → {∗}, which affects physical reality in some way (see Pearl [2009] for a sophisticated discussion of actions and analysis of causality). The final leg of the diagram shows the unfolding of time as it churns the nature of reality itself {∗}→ {∗}, not necessarily in ways we anticipate. If our conceptions are confirmed after a full trip around the loop, we call that *recursive validity*. This is confirmation that conception and action are based in reality, but it is not a guarantee, because it is possible to create a bubble of virtual reality in which the loop seems to function even when it does not. For example, [[property prices only go up]] is self-perpetuating until it is not. More pernicious is the possibility that self-reinforcing "realities" based on observational bias provide false justifications (racism, for example). We see recursive validity as necessary but not sufficient evidence of a well-grounded evaluation and action process.

Connection to the Principles of Evaluation

This epistemic loop in Figure 8.1 is easily connected to the principles of evaluation (American Evaluation Association, 2004). Systematic Inquiry addresses {∗}→ [. . .] concerns, including mereological issues ("make clear the limitations of an evaluation and its results"). Competence applies here as well, because competence is necessary to correctly observe and classify observations and integrate multiple findings into a synthesis. Integrity/Honesty addresses one of the points that can lead to the failure of the epistemic loop—allowing bias to overcome reason. Respect for People as well as Responsibilities for General and Public Welfare encourage sensitivity to parts of the loop that are outside the direct control of the evaluator, namely how stakeholders conceptualize the findings [. . .] → [[. . .]], and the actions that result [[. . .]] → {∗}.

The recursive validity of an epistemic loop is confirmed by ongoing practice. When confirmation fails, we may do an audit of the cycle to see what went wrong. For example, if a university's student affairs office discovers on move-in day that it has more students than beds, a process of error detection would occur. How was the anticipated count created? That is the classification stage {∗}→ [. . .]. Maybe the count was accurate, but the leadership failed to note the importance of it, an issue with the [. . .] → [[. . .]] stage. Or perhaps a maintenance order was poorly timed, and several halls were shut down at a bad moment, a [[. . .]] → {∗}problem. Or it could be that something random happens, like a water leak flooding a residence hall, and the problem is with {∗}→ {∗}. Finally, the report itself may be an error of observation, a flaw with {∗}→ [. . .].

Connection to Validity Theory in Educational Measurement

The field of psychometric validity theory, especially as articulated by Michael Kane (2001), is an evolving epistemological struggle between evidence and assertion that pertains to the observation leg of the recursive validity diagram, resulting in a description. We hope this description is predictive in the sense that we do not really care so much about test results, but we do care about what test results predict about other behaviors; for example, Mary passed the Spanish test, so Mary can ask for directions in Mexico City. Validity theory is related to the principles of evaluation, particularly Systematic Inquiry. Systemization and standardization allow us to assess reliability, which is a window into statistical features of the world. These are often so-called *constructs*, which in the framework we have introduced we would call conceptual, as in [. . . writing score] becomes [[. . . writing abil-ity]]. Kane (2001) gives a historical overview of validity that starts with real-ism, depending on criterion measures, and evolves through mathematically constructed ideals, finally tilting toward social construction of meaning.

Originally, educational testing meant using a convenient method to predict the outcome of an unimpeachable standard—called a criterion—that was less convenient to measure. For example, a test of vocabulary might test only 50 words as a proxy for several thousand. In principle, one could "test the test" by directly examining knowledge of the whole vocab-ulary, but this is often impractical. These criteria generally need to have recursive validity. For example, the SAT exam is tested for predictive value against first-year college grades, and the College Board publishes the results (Wyatt, Kobrin, Proestler, Camara, & Wiley, 2011). Here, the criterion mea-sure is the college grade average at the end of the first year. The report gives information on the *predictive validity* of the test with regard to this criterion. The recursive validity model leads us to ask who it is that con-ceptualizes first-year grades—who cares most about the predictive value of the scores, in other words. The answer is those who set college admissions standards: they generally want to minimize the number of students who do not succeed academically.

Over time criterion-based assessment became replaced with secondary kinds of validity, creating a cottage industry of new statistical approaches. As Kane describes, the reification of test results [. . .] into so-called *constructs* [[. . .]] led to an endorsement of a lower standard for validity than criterion-based assessment (although he does not use such strong language). One problem is that the constructs may be descriptive but not very predictive—without a criterion it is difficult to judge the value of the measurement. Worse, improper use of this approach gives license to start with a concep-tual construct [[. . .]] and create a *post-hoc* test for it. For example, many colleges list *critical thinking* as a learning outcome. This particular outcome is so general as to be nearly meaningless (see Adelman, 2015), with many possible kinds of evidence [[critical thinking]] → {∗}→ [evidence of critical thinking], so that consensus about validity claims is unreachable.

Recursive validity has roots in so-called "consequential" validity. Con-sequential validity is not really validity in the epistemic sense (it is not about some version of *truth*), and some researchers do not like the term (Koretz, 2008, p. 218). Consequential validity is associated with the [[. . .]] → {∗}transduction and the evaluation principles of Respect for Peo-ple and Responsibility for General and Public Welfare. How are the test re-sults being received and used to form actions? What are the consequences of those actions? As such, it is an important part of recursive validity, which entails the whole epistemic cycle in Figure 8.1.

The idea of recursive validity rests on three pillars from validity theory—criterion measures, predictive validity, and consequential validity. First, we insist on criterion measures that are accepted without argument from appropriate stakeholders. This ensures a conceptualization from test results [. . .] to plausible plans for action [[. . .]]. We can think of this as a particular kind of consequential validity. Second, we would like the measure to have predictive validity.

As an example, employers often want to hire college graduates who are proficient with quantitative skills (Association of American Colleges and Universities [AAC&U], 2011). A usual way to address this learning outcome is with a standardized test like the ETS Proficiency Profile. However, this requires the employers to simply believe the claim from the test website that the scores are "valid and actionable" (ETS, 2015). This [test score] → [[graduate can do math]] assumption is problematic because the test score is not a criterion measure (employers do not care about test scores; they care about actual job performance). Instead, suppose we are able to enroll students in internships where they do quantitative work the respective supervisors find authentic. This would be a criterion measure for those employers with [direct observation of student work] → [[student satisfies job requirements]] following. We still require that the quality of student work, as judged by the employer, does not degrade after being hired (predictive validity).

In summary, the epistemic loop for recursive validity of educational outcomes entails the following:

1. [criterion measure] → [[used to plan actions]] is ensured by paying attention to the consequences of matching measures to stakeholders (this is consequential validity, in that irrelevant findings will not be used, but relevant ones will).
2. The execution [[planned actions]] → {∗}→ [criterion measure] demonstrates that the actions had the desired effect (predictive validity).
3. The recursion of this process reinforces the connection between descriptions [. . .] and the real thing {∗}, which creates personal and social conceptions.

The main problem for education assessment is to find criterion measures that are credible to different stakeholders. Most of the usual methods for formative and summative assessment do not meet this requirement.

Assessment of Learning

We focus on student learning outcomes assessment to illuminate one of the most important and challenging problems facing higher education and its evaluation. Despite many advances in the technical aspects of testing, institutions face a credibility gap with the public. The message of *Academically Adrift* is reinforced by a stream of articles in the popular press about how college costs too much, is not worth that price, and the degrees (particularly liberal arts one) are worthless, reifying conclusions like [[higher education is broken]] or more specific conclusions like [[liberal arts are useless]], [[only STEM degrees pay for themselves]], and [[college should be about finding jobs]] (Bump, 2015).

The conceptualization of [...] to [[...]] happens in the minds of individual people, and we are interested in particular categories like students, their parents, higher education professionals, accreditors, employers of graduates, and state and federal elected officials. Each of these will have different biases and favor different kinds of evidence. The Council for Higher Education Accreditation (CHEA) described the assessment challenge as:

> [I]t is imperative for accrediting organizations—as well as the institutions and programs they accredit—to avoid narrow definitions of student learning or excessively standardized measures of student achievement. Collegiate learning is complex, and the evidence used to investigate it must be similarly authentic and contextual. But to pass the test of public credibility—and thus remain faithful to accreditation's historic task of quality assurance—the evidence of student learning outcomes used in the accreditation process must be rigorous, reliable, and understandable. (2003, p. 6)

The implication is that assessments of student learning [...] are intended to pass the test of public credibility [[...]], which is reasonable. But this conflates the roles of observation and conception. It is true that evaluators (in the broadest sense) should base reports on the best information using the best methods. Rigor and reliability are two important considerations in so doing. But a student or parent is not required to conceive of [scored in 95th percentile of a rigorous and reliable test] as [[my degree was worth $50,000 of debt]]. The conception of the value of education is at least as much a personal judgment as it is a scientific deduction. Most institutions of higher learning have a long history of rigorously and reliably tracking credits awarded and grade point averages. But there is a broad consensus that these statistics leave out essential information about student accomplishment. What is easiest to measure may not be the most meaningful.

The glimmer of hope, as with Pandora's box, is the last word fluttering out of the CHEA quotation: understandability. The understandability or meaningfulness of [...] depends on what each stakeholder cares about, not just the statistical properties of the description. For example, if college students prefer [[I will have a good job after graduation]] to [[I have no job after graduation]], then the kind of evidence they are likely to find compelling is [95% of our college's graduates find good jobs within a year of graduation]. The public discourse focuses on just these sorts of outcomes: employment, graduate school acceptance, loan amount, total cost, and so on, and in response to this demand the U.S. Department of Education created a College Scorecard to provide information on jobs, salaries, loans, costs, and dropout rates (collegescorecard.ed.gov). All of these have excellent recursive validity: a graduate with debt will feel the bite of each monthly payment and watch how the principal slowly erodes over time. The numbers on the bank statements are purely abstract, but the effect is palpable and lingering. Test scores or other learning assessments, and even transcripts or diplomas do not make specific claims about the future and therefore have little or no recursive validity from a graduate's point of view. A prospective employer probably will not care much about that "A" in *Modern American Poetry*. The exceptions prove the rule: a nursing license or teacher certification (proxies for learning) do have recursive validity because they open career paths. This does not mean that the qualification exams are necessarily any good at assessing learning, just that passing them has an effect that stakeholders perceive and care about. This impact is an example of *consequential validity* from educational measurement theory (Kane, 2006).

The preceding describes a situation that may be disconcerting to those who work directly with undergraduate students, including course instructors, department and college-level administrators, student affairs, and other support staff. It is difficult to produce rigorous and reliable information about student accomplishment to begin with, but the additional requirement that the stakeholders also need to understand and value that information seems an insurmountable task. It raises the bar for evaluators accordingly. The measures we have cited so far (jobs after graduation and debt, for example) are not outcomes that a course instructor has direct control over. But if parents and employers do not care about test grades, what kind of new evidence can be gathered that aligns learning outcomes and stakeholder values? We call these "authentic outcomes" and describe them in detail in the following section.

Authentic Outcomes

Because stakeholders are increasingly demanding evidence [...] that allows them to answer their important questions [[...]] about students and graduates, the forward-looking principles of evaluation demand that we pay attention. The outcomes of higher education need recursive validity in order to end the current negativity and possible adverse interventions by fed-up lawmakers. This can be addressed only at the program and institutional levels, and this need—and the particulars of that need—should be a priority for evaluators in the name of general and public welfare.

The linchpin of recursive validity is that the purpose of assessment or evaluation is only achieved if stakeholders believe and value the results. The principles of evaluation partially address this in Systematic Inquiry (emphasis added):

Evaluators should communicate their methods and approaches accurately and in sufficient detail to allow others to understand, interpret and critique their work. They should make clear the limitations of an evaluation and its results. Evaluators should discuss in a **contextually appropriate** way those values, assumptions, theories, methods, results, and analyses **significantly affecting the interpretation** of the evaluative findings. These statements apply to all aspects of the evaluation, from its initial conceptualization to the eventual use of findings. (American Evaluation Association, 2004, emphasis added)

The bolded language speaks to the interpretation in context [. . .] → [[. . .]] of stakeholders.

Existing formative methods of learning outcomes assessment, like in-class work, are valuable to the internal stakeholders—teachers and students—but less so for external stakeholders like parents, legislators, or employers. Formative methods may rely on microcriteria like correct use of German grammar, but these cannot be easily aggregated to create a program- or degree-level criterion (despite many efforts and exhortations to the contrary). This is because [Billy scored an 85% on a test of the use of transitive verbs] is not an appropriate observation to give to an employer who is looking for intelligence, writing and speaking ability, and teamwork (AAC&U, 2011), and it comes with no context to usefully conceptualize the score into [[. . .]].

To pass the test of public credibility we cannot depend on the aggregation of test scores or other microcriteria accomplishments that can be usefully conceptualized only in the context of a classroom. Life after college is messy and complex and individual to each student, and the information the public needs cannot be completely standardized. This is anticipated in the literature of assessment:

> An . . . issue related to the reliability of performance-based assessment deals with the trade-off between reliability and validity. As the performance task increases in complexity and authenticity, which serves to increase validity, the lack of standardization serves to decrease reliability. (Palomba & Banta, 1999, p. 89)

Accordingly, we use the term *authentic outcomes* to refer to the complex and possibly individual accomplishments that impress stakeholders. We have already mentioned some of these—finding good jobs, avoiding debt, gaining acceptance to a professional school—which parents of graduates are likely to care about. But there are other public audiences too. An entrepreneur needs customers and a writer needs readers. Authentic outcomes can be found just about everywhere once we start looking for them. In fact, they occur routinely for undergraduates: sports events, artistic performances and shows, service work, scholarly presentation and publication, social activism, and so on. Each of these has a stakeholder audience, which at a minimum must be external to the traditional classroom setting. Work done solely for the classroom is not authentic in this sense, no matter how useful it may be for formative assessment.

External stakeholders together comprise the public, and although there are very many audiences, they are related. A parent who wants a student to find a good job is dependent on the student impressing those doing the hiring. Both are stakeholders, and the authentic outcomes are related. As an example, a computer science graduate who seeks a programming job is more impressive if he or she has a record of authentic outcomes, such as collaborating on open source software projects and a good reputation on Stackoverflow.com, a professional social network for programmers. Thomas Friedman (2014) summed up an interview with a Google hiring manager as, "Beware. Your degree is not a proxy for your ability to do any job. The world only cares about—and pays off on—what you can do with what you know (and it doesn't care how you learned it)" (para. 10).

If this analysis is correct and there is a demand for authentic achievement, we should see suppliers popping up on the Internet, and in fact we do. Kred.com, Klout.com, Predikt.co, and other sites use Internet scanners and machine learning software to create composite scores of job candidates. Predikt.co advertised on its website:

> Our proprietary algorithms learn from patterns, infer implicit skillsets and analyze multiple signals to scientifically determine the Predikt Score. The Score is evaluated based on Job description you create and real industry data we gather by analyzing thousands of other profiles.("Discover your next hire," 2014, para. 3)

The multiple signals referenced comprise information about a candidate that is findable on the Internet, which might include social media, professional activity, portfolios of work, and so on. These services produce findings that may or may not have recursive validity, but their existence shows that there is a demand for [[X is a good fit for this job]], and that college transcripts and diplomas are not sufficient or not entirely trusted. And it points to a solution.

Producing and Describing Authentic Outcomes

Higher education already produces some types of authentic outcomes (performances, internships, etc.), but there is a large gap between the careful documentation of credits and grades and the lack of standardization for documentation of authentic outcomes. This reflects a similar systematic approach to structuring a formal curriculum, but in most cases experiences that can demonstrate real-world skills are left as "cocurricular" options. The classroom walls (real or virtual) implicitly limit "official" education in most programs (visual and performing arts being a notable exception). Historically this was for good reasons. How reasonable is it to expect a beginning mathematics student to meaningfully find and engage an external audience with mathematics? Perhaps by submitting a paper to an undergraduate journal, which is beyond the abilities of most new students. But the Internet has changed this situation by creating low barriers to entry and many forms of engagement. Moreover, electronic media are easily archived and annotated.

As an example of what is now possible, a computer science department with a software development track can show evidence of student collaboration on an open source project via GitHub or SourceForge, activity on Stackoverflow.com, or by creating applications for public use. In 2011 a Stanford University class on developing Facebook apps was so successful that several students started their own companies (Helft, 2011).

In a separate paper (Eubanks & Gliem, 2015), we have given a construction kit for creating and assessing pedagogy that is intended to produce authentic outcomes, comprising these steps:

1. Identify a general topic of interest to the student that can be contextualized by the discipline in question. The work needs to be related to normal teaching and learning.
2. Find a suitable external audience that is already engaged with this topic.
3. Understand the audience needs: style of communication, conventions, and context of the topic (e.g., what is already established and what remains open to investigation).
4. Engage the audience on the topic in a meaningful scalable way, starting with basic interactions. This can (but need not) culminate with higher-order interactions like creation and reception of original content or even creating a new community audience.
5. If the work is deemed useful and authentic, include it in a student's portfolio and the program's portfolio. Use intelligent metadata methods to ensure identifiability and findability of the information in the future. This is the [...] description that can be conceptualized and used by stakeholders.

Here, the engagement of an external audience is the key to authenticity. It models the argument that we have made throughout this chapter, that the ultimate consumers of the educational product should find evidence of accomplishment compelling. This is the test of public credibility, spread over many varieties of the public. An aspiring graphic designer will engage different audiences and produce different kinds of authentic work than an aspiring engineer. Even within these distinctions, each student can customize audiences and interactions to his or her own passions and abilities.

In support of such a program, libraries and teaching/learning centers can be of great help. For an evaluator assessing a program, direct evidence is supported by the means of producing it.

Concluding Remarks

Someone once said that "in theory, theory and practice are the same; in practice they aren't." In 2013 Eckerd College started a pilot program to create class assignments with external audiences using faculty volunteers supported by small institutional grants (subsequently, the project has received support from the Teagle Foundation). Part of the project was to inventory existing practice to see the external audiences already being reached. In addition to the usual ones (performances, internships, conference presentations, etc.), we found that some programs already valued authentic assignments for their pedagogical value. One example is for senior research projects to include a phone interview with one of the authors of their source materials. According to the department chair, the anticipation of interviewing an article's author about the research greatly increased student attention and effort. This was one instance that helped us realize that such engagement is good for documenting authentic outcomes and is independently valuable as good pedagogy.

One student was offered a job directly because of an externally facing project. In a different assignment, a psychology class created a research-based hydration awareness campaign on campus (the college is in Florida). As a result of a calculus class project, a student surveyed traffic patterns on campus, gave a report to the campus safety council, and was invited to become a member of the group. They used her recommendations to make changes to speed bumps.

We found that it can be difficult to make the mental switch from traditional classwork to externally facing assignments, but when the possibilities become apparent it opens up a whole new range of teaching methods. Ironically, technological innovations in education mostly center on online course delivery, which simply replicates the classroom to the cloud. The unnoticed revolution is the lowering of the barriers that used to exist between undergraduates and their impact on the world.

For evaluators working with faculty or staff in higher education, a shift to value the "big picture" represented by recursive validity is simultaneously challenging and exciting. This shift is an intentional move from "reality created by local assumptions" to "reality as defined by stakeholders." Here again technology represents unprecedented access to those stakeholders. As a specific example, consider a forward-looking study abroad office that already takes student learning serious and uses pre/post surveys (e.g., Global Perspective Inventory) or reflective essays to capture changes to student dispositions related to human culture. The next step might be to displace the point of view to that of the ultimate consumers of this experience. How

NEW DIRECTIONS FOR EVALUATION • DOI: 10.1002/ev

could the experience be documented in such a way as to illuminate student abilities? There are many possibilities: teamwork, writing in various genres, photography, discipline knowledge, and so on. A video log of a student leading the digging of a new well in a parched third-world location could be conceptualized as evidence of useful skills by any number of external stakeholders.

At the institutional level, there is currently a lack of intentional creation and archiving of authentic outcomes (cocurricular transcripts notwithstanding). If new graduates were sent on their way not with just a diploma, but with the skills and habits of mind that led them to curate lifelong professional portfolios, everyone would benefit. This skill gives the graduate control over his or her own [...] descriptions, which can be conceptualized by any number of audiences and stakeholders. Tracking and archiving authentic outcomes would also allow the institution to measure and promote the success of its own students in new ways and use that information for recruitment, improvement, and accountability. The challenges to implementing this are cultural, not technological.

In summary, the intent of this discussion of "recursive validity" is to broaden the scope of evaluation in order to uncover new opportunities in higher education. Our system also gives evaluators a vocabulary to be analytical about the important [...] → [[...]] conceptualization step by enlarging the conception of measurement validity. As such, this is an evolutionary, rather than revolutionary, proposal, and one that is in many cases tied to the concurrent advances in technology that allow for greater engagement with geographically scattered audiences and stakeholders. Finally, the proposal is a gentle push back against the technology-fueled trend toward data abstraction as the lodestone of knowledge. In the end, we should not lose the perspective that it is what individual human beings conceive of and care about that leads to decisions.

References

Adelman, C. (2015, February). *To imagine a verb: The language and syntax of learning outcomes statements* (Occasional Paper No. 24). Champaign, IL: National Institute for Learning Outcomes Assessment, University of Illinois at Urbana-Champaign.

American Evaluation Association. (2004). *American Evaluation Association guiding principles for evaluators*. Retrieved from http://www.eval.org/p/cm/ld/fid=51

Arum, R., & Roksa, J. (2011). *Academically adrift: Limited learning on college campuses*. Chicago, IL: University of Chicago Press.

Association of American Colleges and Universities. (2011). *The LEAP vision for learning*. Retrieved from http://www.aacu.org/sites/default/files/files/LEAP/leap_vision_summary.pdf

Bennett, M. R., & Hacker, P. M. S. (2003). *Philosophical foundations of neuroscience*. Hoboken, NJ: Blackwell Publishing.

Bump, P. (2015, February 4). Scott Walker moved to drop "search for truth" from the University of Wisconsin mission. His office claims it was an error. Retrieved from http://www.washingtonpost.com/blogs/the-fix/wp/2015/02/04/scott-walker-wants-to-drop-search-for-truth-from-the-university-of-wisconsin-mission-heres-why/

Council for Higher Education Accreditation. (2003, September). *Statement of mutual responsibilities for student learning outcomes: Accreditation, institutions, and programs.* Retrieved from http://www.chea.org/pdf/StmntStudentLearningOutcomes9-03.pdf

Discover your next hire. (2014, December 18). Retrieved from http://www.predikt.co/

ETS. (2015). *ETS® Proficiency Profile.* Retrieved from https://www.ets.org/proficiency profile/about

Eubanks, D. A., & Gliem, D. E. (2015). *Improving teaching, learning, and assessment by making evidence of achievement transparent* (Occasional Paper No. 25). Champaign, IL: National Institute for Learning Outcomes Assessment, University of Illinois at Urbana-Champaign.

Friedman, T. L. (2014, February 22). How to get a job at Google. *New York Times.* Retrieved from http://www.nytimes.com/2014/02/23/opinion/sunday/friedman-how-to-get-a-job-at-google.html

Helft, M. (2011, May 7). The class that built apps, and fortunes. *The New York Times.* Retrieved from http://www.nytimes.com/2011/05/08/technology/08class.html

Kane, M. T. (2001). Current concerns in validity theory. *Journal of Educational Measurement. 38*(4), 319–342.

Kane, M. T. (2006). Validity. In R. L. Brennan (Ed.), *Educational measurement* (4th ed., pp. 17–59). Westport, CT: Praeger.

Koretz, D. M. (2008). *Measuring up.* Cambridge, MA: Harvard University Press.

Palomba, C. A., & Banta, T. W. (1999). *Assessment essentials: Planning, implementing, and improving assessment in higher education.* San Francisco, CA: Jossey-Bass.

Pearl, J. (2009). *Causality: Models, reasoning and inference.* Cambridge, MA: MIT Press.

Trivers, R. (2011). *The folly of fools: The logic of deceit and self-deception in human life.* New York, NY: Basic Books.

Wyatt, J. N., Kobrin, J. L., Proestler, N., Camara, W. J., & Wiley, A. (2011). *SAT benchmarks: Development of a college readiness benchmark and its relationship to secondary and postsecondary school performance.* New York: College Board. Retrieved from http://research.collegeboard.org/publications/content/2012/05/sat-benchmarks-development-college-readiness-benchmark-and-its

DAVID EUBANKS *is the assistant vice president of assessment and institutional research at Furman University.*

DAVID GLIEM *is an associate professor of art history at Eckerd College.*

Stitt-Bergh, M., Rickards, W. H., & Jones, T. B. (2016). Beyond the rhetoric: Evaluation practices in higher education. In W. H. Rickards, & M. Stitt-Bergh (Eds.), *Evaluating student
learning in higher education: Beyond the public rhetoric. New Directions for Evaluation*, 151,
123–132.

9

Beyond the Rhetoric: Evaluation Practices in Higher Education

Monica Stitt-Bergh, William H. Rickards, Tamara Bertrand Jones

Abstract

*North American higher education institutions have been developing their own
systems of learning outcomes assessment that are not part of the public rhetoric
on higher education. Evaluators have new opportunities in higher education and
evaluator–faculty partnerships are a key to their success. Evaluator knowledge
of the institution-specific context and evaluator cultural competence can help
evaluators overcome faculty resistance and design appropriate assessment systems. In higher education, the evaluators' roles include documenting and facilitating use of results, leveraging technology and existing data, negotiating what
becomes public information, and coauthoring with faculty.* © 2016 Wiley Periodicals, Inc., and the American Evaluation Association.

> We're in a tricky, troubling spot. At a time when our nation's ability to tackle
> complicated policy problems is seriously in doubt, we must pull off a delicate
> balancing act. We must make college practical but not excessively so, lower
> its price without lowering its standards and increase the number of diplomas
> attained without diminishing not only their currency in the job market but
> also the fitness of the country's work force in a cutthroat world.
>
> Frank Bruni, *New York Times* Op-Ed (October 12, 2013, para. 14)

New Directions for Evaluation, no. 151, Fall 2016 © 2016 Wiley Periodicals, Inc., and the American Evaluation
Association.   Published online in Wiley Online Library (wileyonlinelibrary.com) • DOI: 10.1002/ev.20203

123

T he public rhetoric and certain education policies in the United States have colored perceptions of evaluation and assessment in higher education, often narrowing the purpose to high-stakes accountability for individuals and institutions and not to guide advancement of programs to better serve changing societal needs and diverse student populations. *Time* magazine, *The New York Times*, *The Wall Street Journal*, and the Public Broadcasting Service have captured some of the challenges associated with an accountability model: Given the many types of institutions and programs—technical, professional, liberal arts programs—and a diverse student population with all income classes, all levels of academic preparation, all ages, and varying prior college and work experiences, an agreement on the student knowledge, competencies, and/or values that should be evaluated so that colleges can be held accountable and compared is indefinable. Yet, attempts to do so persist.

The effects of *No Child Left Behind* (U.S. Department of Education, 2001) on elementary and secondary schools reverberated through higher education and brought to the forefront the threat of using students' standardized test scores to evaluate institutional quality and impose sanctions. In higher education, the Spellings Commission report, *A Test of Leadership: Charting the Future of U.S. Higher Education* (U.S. Department of Education, 2006), included a recommendation for a public database of colleges and universities with information on their students' learning as measured by standardized exams, time to degree, and retention and graduation rates. In 2013, the U.S. Department of Education announced its plan to develop the Postsecondary Institutional Ratings System and use the results to evaluate institutions and to allocate student financial aid to campuses. With 133.8 billion U.S. government dollars in financial aid distributed in 2014 to undergraduate and graduate students at over 6,000 institutions (Federal Student Aid, 2014), such an evaluation system would be high stakes for campuses. But after a year and a half of difficult work involving many stakeholders to establish outcomes and indicators, the Department of Education backed away from a rating system and created a public information system, the College Scorecard (https://collegescorecard.ed.gov/) that went online in fall 2015.

North American higher education institutions have been developing their own systems of learning outcomes assessment while keeping an eye on the discussions and proposals by the federal government and accrediting organizations to change reporting requirements and accompanying carrots and sticks for compliance. In this New Directions for Evaluation (NDE) issue, the contributors described some of those efforts and offered a look into evaluation practices that are new to higher education, namely, program learning outcomes assessment. Their approaches emphasize assessment for improvement, particularly student learning improvement. Analysis of the main concepts in this issue—partnerships, meaningful engagement, satisfying multiple audiences, and the use of results for improvement—leads us

NEW DIRECTIONS FOR EVALUATION • DOI: 10.1002/ev

to optimistic and interesting avenues for outcomes assessment in and out of higher education. What is happening in higher education assessment is more than the rhetoric. In this chapter, we tie together the main concepts and what we have learned with an eye toward the future.

Evaluator and Faculty Partnerships: The Necessity of Meaningful Engagement

Evaluator–faculty partnerships effectively combat common reasons that outcomes assessment does not take place. In general, faculty are not willing to participate in evaluation for evaluation's sake or only to satisfy external compliance requirements, but they are willing to have useful, productive conversations about student learning. The burden of proof that outcomes assessment is beneficial falls on the evaluator's shoulders. Through trust building and an evaluator's willingness to learn from faculty about disciplinary conventions, evaluators can partner with faculty and overcome skepticism and reluctance to engage.

Faculty participation in assessment is crucial. Colleges and universities face the daunting task of program outcomes assessment in the context of limited resources: state funding of higher education in the United States is down an average of 20% (Mitchell & Leachman, 2015). Although they can hire evaluators to assist with the process, the number will likely not be enough. Public, 4-year campuses may have over 150 different academic programs that need ongoing assistance. An evaluator–faculty partnership helps manage the workload through shared responsibilities, capacity building, and communities of practice.

The chapters in this issue by Tesch, Secolsky et al., and Eubanks and Gliem foreground technical evaluation expertise as a necessary element in the evaluator–faculty partnership and indicate the challenging responsibility of communicating the technicalities. Because the design constrains interpretation and the data do not speak for themselves, the evaluator as collaborator and facilitator can help guide, from planning to appropriate use of findings. The skilled effort needed is complicated by the length of the typical project—the projects described in this issue spanned years—and the constant change of people as faculty and student schedules changed, committee terms ended, and administrations changed.

Campuses want to simultaneously satisfy various audiences who have a stake in higher education: students, faculty, administration, community, and external agencies. Despite the importance of each group, external mandates by regional and professional accreditation are the primary drivers of learning outcomes assessment, followed by institutional improvement and faculty interest in improving student learning (Kuh, Jankowski, Ikenberry, & Kinzie, 2014). The challenge for evaluators is to develop assessment systems that privilege faculty interest in student learning and the desire for institutional improvement such that a natural byproduct from the

NEW DIRECTIONS FOR EVALUATION • DOI: 10.1002/ev

assessment activities is the documentation needed by external agencies. Additionally, although the conversations about data and measurement are important, they must be part of the meaning making and sense making that are critical to evaluation reasoning (Davidson, 2012; Patton, 2012). Four chapters in this issue (Parsons et al., Rickards et al., Stevenson et al., & Stitt-Bergh) explicated successful systems in which evaluators supported faculty conversations about student learning and outcomes assessment in ways that could be documented and used as evidence for external agencies.

Evaluators' Skill, Cultural Competence, and Contextual Knowledge

The "assessment movement" in higher education provides a positive outlook for evaluators interested in working in higher education. It is a significant departure from traditional assessment (e.g., course grades and standardized testing). Colleges and universities know they need to produce and use evidence to satisfy internal and external audiences. Although these institutions may not be able to employ a sufficient number of evaluators, they are hiring (an average of seven job announcements were posted per month on the ASSESS listserv in 2015, http://lsv.uky.edu/archives/assess.html). Collaborating and partnering with faculty in ways we have seen in the previous chapters take more than textbook knowledge. Colleges need evaluators with a combination of evaluation technical knowledge and interpersonal skills, familiarity with the higher education context, and cultural competence. Next, we describe implications of success and illustrate trends for evaluators interested in or already working in higher education.

Evaluators' Technical Knowledge and Interpersonal Skills Result in Access to Leadership and Influence

Evaluation technical knowledge aids an evaluator's ability to contribute to decision making via high-quality information that supports or challenges claims of learning and program impact. Evaluators' contributions to decision making provide them with access to decision makers that can result in power and influence with said decision makers. Misused power and influence cause fear, misunderstanding, and even hostility from faculty and administrators—the very individuals whom assessment and evaluation seek to serve. Technically, competent evaluators acknowledge the influence that comes with being able to use data to tell the story of learning or development, and they embrace the potential for leadership that develops out of proximity to faculty leaders and administrators. The conversations that evaluators take part in provide them opportunities to address issues of equity, access, and success for different student populations, and using the data and meaning making generated from evaluation and assessment activities, evaluators can discuss disappointing findings and support effective

New Directions for Evaluation • DOI: 10.1002/ev

practices. In some cases, their unique function may be to document the developing discourse among the educators and allow the community to reflect on its progress.

Evaluators' Knowledge of Contextual Factors in Higher Education Is a Key to Their Success

Evaluators doing assessment work in higher education can better work within this setting if they have a broad understanding of higher education organizations. Understanding of the varying models of higher education and the ways those models influence institutional organization and governance, as well as institutional culture, is especially important. For example, institution-specific knowledge can include the following: percentage of part-time faculty (including graduate teaching assistants); percentage of tenure/tenure-track faculty; amount of faculty autonomy in regard to teaching; the role of a faculty union and/or faculty contracts; the percentage of faculty work expected for teaching, research, and service; the views on academic freedom; the campus governance model (e.g., "shared governance"); whether the campus is an indigenous-serving institution; the percentage of face-to-face, hybrid, online, and other instructional settings. These campus characteristics have great impact on faculty willingness and ability to engage in assessment activities and thus on the selection of the most appropriate evaluation approach/model and the role of evaluator.

Knowing, respecting, and using the institution's past efforts and historical documents can save time and demonstrate trust in faculty expertise. A common suggestion in the assessment literature and a widespread practice is the use of existing evidence of learning such as course assignments, exams, and projects ("embedded assessment") because student motivation and faculty engagement are high. Two other sets of useful historical documents are campus survey results (including the National Survey of Student Engagement and alumni surveys) and committee reports. Finally, when thinking about design and use of findings, structural constraints from previous agreements among stakeholders may limit the scope and options (e.g., the multicampus agreement on degree requirements as seen in Tesch's chapter in this issue). An evaluator's knowledge of these contextual dimensions at an institution and higher education more broadly contribute to understanding what frameworks, models, or other components of the assessment process will work best for the institution and program of focus.

Evaluators' Cultural Competence Lends Credibility to Their Work

The American Evaluation Association's (2004) *Guiding Principles for Evaluators* and *Public Statement on Cultural Competence in Evaluation* (2011) highlight the importance of evaluators' competence in engaging contextual and cultural dimensions in evaluation practice. The principles outlined by the association identify core concepts that are central to evaluators' cultural competence. First, culture is fundamental to larger social systems (i.e., educational, political) and individual identity and thus a significant contributor to the assessment in higher education. The acknowledgement of the various dimensions of institutional culture mentioned previously is integral to the validity and credibility of an evaluation. Culturally, competent evaluation is good evaluation!

Another principle of cultural competence in evaluation is the evaluator's acknowledgement that culture is fluid and may result in observable (or nonobservable) phenomena in different contexts with different student populations. Evaluators possess the knowledge and skills to help faculty and campus administrators ask questions that explain differing perspectives and experiences. For example, in a study of campus climate, questions about the institution's long-standing tradition of homecoming resulted in different perceptions based on student group membership (Bertrand Jones et al., 2014). Whereas a majority of students embraced the opportunity to experience the institution's football culture, students from underrepresented racial/ethnic groups expressed isolation and discrimination in an event thought to bring the entire campus together. Similar disaggregation of information is needed with program- and institutional-level learning outcomes assessment.

Last, cultural competence necessitates an evaluator's self-awareness to identify how his or her social location, skills, and life experiences may influence the quality of the evaluation process. Attention to interpersonal skills not only ensures that evaluators are equipped with the skills to develop those trusting relationships mentioned previously but also contribute directly and indirectly to the quality of the data collection and analysis processes. For example, evaluator-development opportunities can encourage cultural competence, including interpersonal skills such as facilitation, conflict mediation, listening, understanding nonverbal cues, emotional intelligence, and empathy. Together, cultural competence, evaluation technical skills, and knowledge of the higher education context equip evaluators to contribute in positive ways to assessment in higher education. In the next section, we identify trends for evaluators in higher education.

Evaluators' Roles in Higher Education Assessment

The changes in external reporting requirements and campuses' internal emphases on using evaluative information about students and learning for improvement purposes have generated new opportunities for evaluators in higher education. Next, we highlight new evaluation needs in higher education and the potential roles for evaluators.

Internal Evaluators May Be Ideal to Meet Quality Demands

In higher education, the accreditor plays a role similar to that of a funder in other evaluation situations. When a funder asks for certain outcomes and

NEW DIRECTIONS FOR EVALUATION • DOI: 10.1002/ev

types of evaluation, the fund recipient and evaluator meet those terms. It is no different in higher education, except that the regional accreditation agencies have stipulated that faculty (the program personnel) be involved in the assessment process, that faculty use the results, and that the assessment be ongoing. Interestingly, the regional accreditors, at this time, are less concerned with the documentation of the actual amount of learning and more concerned with institutions being "learning organizations" and attending to technical evaluation issues (e.g., reliability). Internal evaluators can build trust, lasting relationships, and assist over time, which are all needed in higher education to meaningfully meet external demands.

Evaluator–faculty partnerships and the long length of study for assessment projects make an internal evaluator an ideal choice. An evaluator who is familiar with the campus is more likely to provide the safe and comfortable space needed for hesitant or doubting faculty. In addition, internal evaluators can also be present during new program planning, which increases the likelihood that assessment can be meaningfully integrated and not an afterthought. A long-term investment is needed. We foresee an increasing role for the internal evaluator in higher education.

Evaluators Can Help Bring in "Big Data"

Coordinating data from multiple sources will be vital to a comprehensive understanding of program impact. As in other evaluation contexts, advances in technology systems have increased the amount of accessible data. Eubanks and Gliem (this issue) touch upon this when they discuss social media and its possibilities for authentic forms of learning assessment and data collection. Companies have developed cloud-based apps to facilitate data collection and analysis that make new interpretations and uses possible. Campuses already have much data on students that can be used to aid interpretations of learning assessment results. Evaluators in higher education can collaborate with others on campus to analyze learning outcome results in terms of student demographics, college preparation, financial aid, course-taking patterns, etc. It is also useful to link with related national efforts (e.g., Bienkowski, Feng, & Means, 2012; Pascarella & Blaich, 2013; State Higher Education Executive Officers Association, 2015). At the least, evaluators can assist the institution in discovering if there are patterns of achievement by key demographics (e.g., ethnicity and financial status) so the institution can address equity outcomes and succeed for students in all groups.

Evaluators Assist with "Closing the Loop" and Documenting Use

Action on results is the primary goal of assessment in higher education, and thus assessment reports need to include what actions were taken after results were presented. In contrast, a traditional evaluation report can end with an interpretation of results and a discussion of planned use and planned dissemination. In higher education, follow-up documentation is needed that describes what the program did and the rationale for the actions. In the assessment literature, this is referred to as "closing the loop" and it reinforces the assessment-for-improvement model and satisfies internal and external audience demands. Faculty look to evaluators for assistance in use of results or in locating appropriate experts to guide them.

Similar to other evaluation contexts, use of findings remains difficult (Blaich & Wise, 2011; Kuh & Ikenberry, 2009). However, faculty who participate in assessment activities—whether it be discussing learning outcomes, developing tools, interpreting findings—learn about teaching and the curriculum, and they do report changes to their own teaching and/or the program. The evaluator–faculty partnership is the catalyst and we encourage evaluators to monitor and document such changes.

Thus, as the shift to use of results occurs, evaluation research can play a role. Specifically, to what extent does participation in assessment lead to changes in teaching and subsequent student learning? Does mandated use and privileging of use increase the likelihood of use? Or, do difficulties associated with use of results continue? For evaluators interested in evaluation use, college campuses provide a new setting for research in this area. And as more is learned about facilitating the discussions around data, meaning making, and educator practice, what are the implications for preparation and development for evaluator expertise?

Evaluators Can Help Faculty and Campuses Negotiate What Will Become Public

Calls for transparency in higher education continue. Evaluators can expect to address calls for public presentation of assessment results. Secolsky et al. (this issue) address some of the measurement difficulties and challenges that need to be considered, especially if results will be public. Campuses and faculty question whether assessment should be a public activity and which results should be public. Full disclosure can change the dynamic and reliability of the process, especially in cases with negative findings and few institutional resources to carry out desired improvements. Institutions need help, and already-forged trust relationships with evaluators will aid the negotiations.

Evaluators Can Partner with Faculty to Publish and Present

The higher education assessment literature already has descriptions of what campuses are doing; evaluators can contribute to the literature by adding evaluation frameworks to help campuses have language and theory for what they are doing. The evaluation literature and the assessment literature have not intersected: both have much to gain by sharing and examining each other's practices, which grew from different roots despite many similarities.

The chapters in this NDE issue reflect the developing role of evaluators as they serve institutions engaged in studying their own educational practices. They place importance on the evaluators' capacity to support the deliberative work of faculty, staff, and administrators, and that is a process equally as important as managing the technical aspects of evaluation. From improving measurement expertise to supporting the discourse of educators, to joining the issues of access and equity with learning and educational practice, these chapters offer new perspectives on evaluators' roles in current and emerging issues in higher education.

References

American Evaluation Association. (2004). *American Evaluation Association guiding principles for evaluators*. Fairhaven, MA: Author. Retrieved from http://www.eval.org

American Evaluation Association. (2011). *American Evaluation Association public statement on cultural competence in evaluation*. Fairhaven, MA: Author. Retrieved from http://www.eval.org

Bertrand Jones, T., Pelzer, D., Gerbers, K., Chunoo, V., Hernandez, E., Hunt, J., . . . Wu, Y. (2014). *Identity and inclusion: A campus climate study*. Tallahassee, FL: Florida State University.

Bienkowski, M., Feng, M., & Means, B. (2012). *Enhancing teaching and learning through educational data mining and learning analytics: An issue brief*. Washington, DC: U.S. Department of Education, Office of Educational Technology.

Blaich, C., & Wise, K. (2011). *From gathering to using assessment results: Lessons from the Wabash national study* (Occasional Paper 8). Champaign, IL: National Institute for Learning Outcomes Assessment. Retrieved from http://www.learningoutco meassessment.org/occasionalpapereight.htm

Bruni, F. (2013, October 12). College's identity crisis. *New York Times*. Retrieved from http://www.nytimes.com/2013/10/13/opinion/sunday/bruni-colleges-identity-crisis. html

Davidson, J. (2012). Why "*What's the best tool to measure the effectiveness of X?*" is *the wrong question*. Retrieved from http://genuineevaluation.com/whats-the-best-tool-wrong-question

Federal Student Aid. (2014). *Annual report FY 2014*. Washington, DC: U.S. Department of Education. Retrieved from https://www2.ed.gov/about/reports/annual/2014 report/fsa-report.pdf

Kuh, G. D., & Ikenberry, S. (2009). *More than you think, less than we need: Learning outcomes assessment in American higher education*. Champaign, IL: National Institute for Learning Outcomes Assessment. Retrieved from http://www.learningoutcome assessment.org/NILOAsurveyresults09.htm

Kuh, G. D., Jankowski, J., Ikenberry, S. O., & Kinzie, J. (2014). *Knowing what students know and can do: The current state of learning outcomes assessment in U.S. colleges and universities*. Champaign, IL: National Institute for Learning Outcomes Assessment. Retrieved from http://www.learningoutcomesassessment.org/documents/ 2013%20Survey%20Report%20Final.pdf

Mitchell, M., & Leachman, M. (2015, May 13). *Years of cuts threaten to put college out of reach for more students*. Center on Budget and Policy Priorities. Retrieved from http://www.cbpp.org/research/state-budget-and-tax/years-of-cuts-threaten-to-put-col lege-out-of-reach-for-more-students

Pascarella, E. T., & Blaich, C. (2013). Lessons from the Wabash National Study of Liberal Arts Education. *Change: The Magazine of Higher Learning. 45*(2), 6–15.

Patton, M. Q. (2012). Contextual pragmatics of valuing. In G. Julnes (Ed.), *New Directions for Evaluation: No. 133. Promoting valuation in the public interest: Informing policies for judging value in evaluation* (pp. 97–108). San Francisco, CA: Jossey-Bass.

State Higher Education Executive Officers Association. (2015). *MSC: A Multistate Collaborative to Advance Learning Outcomes Assessment.* Retrieved from http://www.sheeo.org/projects/msc-multi-state-collaborative-advance-learning-outcomes-assessment

U.S. Department of Education. (2001). *No Child Left Behind Act of 2001.* Retrieved from http://www2.ed.gov/policy/elsec/leg/esea02/index.html

U.S. Department of Education (2006). *A test of leadership: Charting the future of U.S. higher education.* Retrieved from http://www2.ed.gov/about/bdscomm/list/hiedfuture/reports/pre-pub-report.pdf

MONICA STITT-BERGH is an associate specialist of assessment at the University of Hawai'i at Mānoa.

WILLIAM H. RICKARDS is a consultant at Independent Evaluation Inquiry.

TAMARA BERTRAND JONES is an assistant professor of higher education and the associate director of the Center for Postsecondary Success at Florida State University.

INDEX

133

ORDER FORM SUBSCRIPTION AND SINGLE ISSUES

DISCOUNTED BACK ISSUES:

Use this form to receive 20% off all back issues of *New Directions for Evaluation*.
All single issues priced at **$23.20** (normally $29.00)

TITLE	ISSUE NO.	ISBN

Call 1-800-835-6770 or see mailing instructions below. When calling, mention the promotional code JBNND to receive your discount. For a complete list of issues, please visit www.wiley.com/WileyCDA/WileyTitle/productCd-EV.html

SUBSCRIPTIONS: (1 YEAR, 4 ISSUES)

☐ New Order   ☐ Renewal

U.S.	☐ Individual: $89	☐ Institutional: $380
Canada/Mexico	☐ Individual: $89	☐ Institutional: $422
All Others	☐ Individual: $113	☐ Institutional: $458

Call 1-800-835-6770 or see mailing and pricing instructions below.
Online subscriptions are available at www.onlinelibrary.wiley.com

ORDER TOTALS:

Issue / Subscription Amount: $ _____

Shipping Amount: $ _____
(for single issues only – subscription prices include shipping)

Total Amount: $ _____

SHIPPING CHARGES:

First Item $6.00
Each Add'l Item $2.00

(No sales tax for U.S. subscriptions. Canadian residents, add GST for subscription orders. Individual rate subscriptions must be paid by personal check or credit card. Individual rate subscriptions may not be resold as library copies.)

BILLING & SHIPPING INFORMATION:

☐ **PAYMENT ENCLOSED:** *(U.S. check or money order only. All payments must be in U.S. dollars.)*

☐ **CREDIT CARD:**   ☐ VISA   ☐ MC   ☐ AMEX

Card number _____ Exp. Date _____

Card Holder Name_____ Card Issue # _____

Signature _____ Day Phone _____

☐ **BILL ME:** *(U.S. institutional orders only. Purchase order required.)*

Purchase order # _____
Federal Tax ID 13559302 • GST 89102-8052

Name_____

Address_____

Phone_____ E-mail_____

Copy or detach page and send to: **John Wiley & Sons, Inc. / Jossey Bass**
PO Box 55381
Boston, MA 02205-9850

PROMO JBNND